Wings Across America

WINGS ACROSS

BRUCE MCALLISTER
AND JESSE DAVIDSON

ROUNDUP PRESS
BOULDER, COLORADO, U.S.A.

AMERICA

*A Photographic History
of the U. S. Air Mail*

© 2004 by Bruce McAllister and Jesse Davidson

All rights reserved. No part of this book may be reproduced, stored in a retrieval system or transmitted in any form or by any means without written permission of the publisher.

Roundup Press, P.O. Box 109, Boulder, CO 80306-0109

Library of Congress Control Number 2003095569
ISBN 0-9638817-9-5

BOOK DESIGN
Paulette Livers, Livers Lambert Design, Boulder, CO
PHOTO EDITOR
Bruce McAllister

PHOTO CREDITS
Front cover: Jesse Davidson Aviation Archives
Back Cover: ©Captain A. W. Stevens/Jesse Davidson Aviation Archives

Printed and bound in China by C&C Offset Printing Co., ltd.

DISCLAIMER
The authors have attempted to give accurate aeronautical information. They cannot be held responsible for the accuracy of this information and it is not to be used for navigational purposes.

SPECIAL THANKS TO
Bette Davidson Kalash of the Jesse Davidson Aviation Archives

ACKNOWLEDGMENTS
Joyce Adgate, Centre County Library, Bellefonte, PA
Noel Allard, Minnesota Aviation Hall of Fame
Caroline Atuk, University of Alaska, Fairbanks
Dick Bevington
Lee Brumbaugh, Nevada Historical Society
Bob Burns
Jim Davis
Barbara Hansen, United Airlines Archives
Donald B. Holmes
Amber Johns and Jan Peterson, North East Nevada Historical Society
Keith Lambertsen
Ruth Lauritzen, Sweetwater County Museum, Green River, WY
Lufthansa Photo Archives, Hamburg, Germany
J. Willard Marriott Library, University of Utah
Montana Historical Society
Union Pacific Railroad
Vern Predoehl
John Rutter, National Geographic Society
Stella de Sa Rego, Center For Southwest Research, University of New Mexico
Earl Shobe
Gabriel Sperling, Franklin County Historical Museum, Pasco, WA
State Historical Society of Iowa
Gary Valentine, Rock Springs Airport, Rock Springs, WY
Doyle Werner, North Platte Historical Committee, North Platte, NE
Katherine Williams, Museum of Flight, Seattle
Nancy Allison Wright, Air Mail Pioneers

ALSO AVAILABLE FROM ROUNDUP PRESS:
Wings Above the Arctic ISBN 0-9638817-8-7 $39.95(Add $5.00 for P&H)
Wings Over The Alaska Highway   ISBN 0-9638817-7-9 $34.95(Add $5.00 for P&H)

In memory of Jesse Davidson (1913-1983)

Dad's early interest in the air mail began when, as a youngster growing up at an orphanage in Westchester County, New York, he would fling open the windows of the dormitory at the sound of an approaching airplane that came over the "home" several nights a week around nine o'clock. The aircraft was flying very low! They eventually learned that it was a Pitcairn Mailwing on a regular schedule from Newark to Boston.

Soon the orphanage formed an aviation club to spur the interest of the boys in learning more about "aeroplanes." Dad devoured everything on the subject–books, magazines, aircraft models. As he later wrote, "Over the years, we witnessed the familiar biplane give way to the monoplane carrying both passengers and mail. And we marveled at Lindbergh's famous solo Trans-Atlantic flight. But none of us youngsters had ever seen a real airplane on the ground. One mid-summer Sunday, a friend and I sneaked off the premises and hiked from Yonkers to New Rochelle where, I had learned, there was a landing field. As we neared the large open area, we heard a whirring sound, looked up, and saw a large silver and blue biplane swooping low as it landed."

"Soon we saw the airplane parked between tall trees. The small shack that served as an office was empty. At first we stood in silent awe at a respectful distance, but suddenly we broke loose and ran up to the plane. Taking another quick look around the deserted field, I climbed into the cockpit. The instruments, the switch, the throttle, the control stick, and rudder pedals–Wow! I moved the control stick right and left, forward and back, watched the ailerons and rudder and elevators respond to my touch…I peered closer to read a nameplate, which identified the airplane as an Eaglerock. I sat there taking in all the sights and smells of the leather padding, the freshly doped and painted surfaces of a newly manufactured aircraft."

Not long after leaving the orphanage, Dad was brought to the attention of Bernard McFadden, owner of *Model Airplane News* and *Flying Stories*. "I was an instructor in free model building and also designed and provided instructions on how to build and fly certain models, which were published in each month's edition of *Model Airplane News*."

The Depression years of the thirties delayed his plans to fly, but near the end of that decade, he did learn in a Piper Cub. His flying instructor was Frederic Ives Lord, a World War I ace, who had recently returned from flying combat missions for the Loyalists in the Spanish Civil War.

Eventually Lord soloed him in the Piper J-3 Cub and he became a pilot. In the thirties, Dad was a writer on the staff of *Flying Aces*, taking over as editor until he entered military service in World War II. He later authored a book, *Famous Firsts of Aviation*, and served as the leading consultant on Time-Life's *Flying The Mail*. In retirement, he traveled throughout the country, interviewing many of the air mail pioneers and collecting their photographs.

—Bette Davidson Kalash
Great Neck, New York
May, 2003

In the Cockpit with Jack Knight...

The following excerpts (courtesy of United Airlines) are from the memoirs of Jack Knight, the air mail pilot who flew the memorable night air mail flight from North Platte, Nebraska, to Chicago on February 22, 1921. Before his retirement from United Airlines in 1937, Knight flew more than 417,000 air route miles for the Air Mail Service and can arguably be considered the most daring and resourceful of the pioneer air mail pilots.

"Don't think that we early pilots were sissies—perish the thought! Contest flying was distinctly our dish. It was no disgrace nor dishonor to crack up an airplane, attempting an impossible flight in bad weather, but to ever return to a starting base, and admit a weather defeat, was disgrace, dishonor, and good grounds for separation from service.

Remember, we had no instruments for blind flight—no two-way radio, nor any of the remarkable safety devices that are in daily use on the Air Transcontinental Systems today.

The original band of U.S. Air Mail Pilots (twenty in number) were the most experienced group of pilots to be found in the world at that time, in 1914. We were attempting to deliver 100% performance, with rebuilt war time material for equipment—with motors that quit with great regularity, and with what was then a wealth of experience gained from three hundred hours of flying." *[From United Airlines Archives, article "It Can't Happen Now," p. 1]*

After arguing against flying in zero visibility weather with the dispatcher in Chicago one foggy night in the 1920s, when "even the birds are walking," Knight had an exciting takeoff on an air mail run to Bellefonte, Pennsylvania.

"After several run-ups, it was time to go. With a hasty glance at the almost invisible wind sock, I gave the signal to pull the blocks, cast a most murderous, malignant look at the old man [the dispatcher], accompanied by a left-hand salute, gunned the motor and picked up speed for the take-off. It was impossible to see over 50 feet ahead of the ship, and knowing that the airport was surrounded by trees and houses, I stalled the ship off at 60 m.p.h. (air speed) and immediately tried to maintain, as closely as possible, 40 feet elevation above the ground. As soon as I attained this attitude, my entire attention was necessary to avoid a collision with housetops, high tension wires, chimneys, etc., which whizzed suddenly out of the thick murky fog at 100 m.p.h. within a few feet of the wings of my craft. Every second a new thrill—forgotten my bitter quarrel with the old man. A minute of regret at my foolhardiness to start what bid fair to be an utterly impossible attempt at a flight.

Crash! A shiver ran through the ship. Branches flew through a wing, a few lodging in the wing wires. Baby! Was that a close call! A tree a bit higher than I had reckoned. No serious damage ... yet. I reached right out and caught my heart, and having recaptured it, crammed it back into my throat. A final blur of housetops and chimneys rushing close under my wings, and I was on the outskirts of the city of Cleveland, Ohio. Now to find an east-west road, and then start following the insulators on the telephone poles. At last, success!! ... I found a road and proceeded, my wing tips even with and parallel to the telephone wires, flying ten or fifteen feet away from them." *[From United Airlines Archives, article "It Can't Happen Now," pp. 3–6]*

On flying a tube of antitoxin (to save the lives of some poison victims) from Chicago to New York City, January 17, 1920, in a twin Martin mail plane (powered by a pair of Liberty 400 engines). On January 15, two days before the planned mercy flight:

"This machine, #205, had a broken tail skid—broken aileron masts on both lower right and left wing ailerons—and many holes punched in the wing coverings and a hole where somebody had stepped through the cover of the rear mail compartment, and neither motor hitting right when Oakes landed at Grant Park."

On January 17, the day of the flight: " ... at 11:30 [a.m.] they said the ship was O.K. and motors functioning fine. I climbed into the cockpit, started both motors; neither tachometer was working and the left motor sounded awfully sour.

They had told me that there was about 600 lbs. of mail on board. I later found 14 sacks, each weighing about 100 lbs. apiece. ... I took off south to north and at 50 ft. elevation discovered my aileron controls were gone. I kept in a straight line, using as best I could my rudder to keep me level. At 200 feet altitude my left motor died to about 1100 r.p.m., letting me settle almost on the roofs of factories north of the field. I ruddered as best I could out over the lake, intending to set down on the ice rather than crash on the roofs of buildings." *[From United Airlines Archives, report dated January 19, 1920]*

CONTENTS

	Foreword	xi
	Introduction	1
Chapter 1	Aeroplane Station No. 1	13
Chapter 2	Katherine Stinson: Air Mail Aviatrix	23
Chapter 3	Liftoff!	31
Chapter 4	From Khakis to Civies	43
Chapter 5	Hell's Stretch: Surviving the Allegheny Mountains	57
Chapter 6	Going West with Nutter	71
Chapter 7	Memorable and Mortal Flights	79
Chapter 8	The First Transcontinental Flight	91

Chapter 9	Flying the Alaska Air Mail	101
Chapter 10	Flying the Mail Through the Night	113
Chapter 11	From Omaha to the Golden Gate	131
Chapter 12	North America's First International Air Mail Flight	153
Chapter 13	Expanding the Contract Air Mail Routes	161
Chapter 14	The Airlines Are Born	175
Chapter 15	Air Mail First-Day Covers	201
	Notes	209
	Bibliography	210
	About the Authors	212

FOREWORD

Wings Across America is an excellent, stirring account—well written and beautifully illustrated—of the romance of America's air mail service. It fully captures the amazing courage and skill of the pilots who carried the mail in bad weather, dangerous flight conditions, and with the most primitive navigation and communication equipment. Death claimed thirty of these pioneering pilots and it rode in the cockpit on nearly every flight—especially those at night in stormy weather.

—George S. McGovern
World War II B-24 pilot who flew
35 combat missions over Europe
and was awarded the Distinguished
Flying Cross. He also was a twenty-
two-year congressman and the 1972
Democratic presidential nominee.

INTRODUCTION

The history of air mail service in the United States is marked by daring, determination, and dedication. The exploits are legendary; the heroes are larger than life.

The story begins in the mid-1800s. At that time, mail was moved across the United States and Europe by balloon. In 1870, during the Franco-Prussian War, besieged but resourceful Parisians found a way to move mail over German lines by balloon. On September 23, 1870, they deployed a large cotton bag filled with coal gas and christened it *Le Neptune*. Helpful prevailing winds carried it westward. After almost four hours of flight, it landed safely near Evreux, about fifty-five miles west-northwest of Paris, in friendly territory. Two hundred and seventy-five pounds of mail were carried by the balloon. This success prompted three more balloon air mail flights. The four flights transported a total of nine hundred pounds of mail.[1]

Opposite: Dirigible LZ-127 Graf Zeppelin *passes over a crowd at the Brandenburg Gate in Berlin, October 1928.*
Lufthansa Photo Archives

Below: Dirigible Graf Zeppelin *in Germany in the 1920s.*
Lufthansa Photo Archives

A de Havilland DH-4 aircraft flying across the Rockies. Date and location unknown. Jesse Davidson Aviation Archives

Seven years later, in the United States, Samuel King made his one-hundredth sixty-ninth flight on June 18, 1877. He flew a balloon named *Buffalo* from Nashville, Tennessee, to Gallatin, Tennessee—a distance of twenty miles. On this flight, for the first time in the United States, privately produced stamps were affixed to mail being transported by air.[2]

In 1894, the first scheduled air mail service in the United States was inaugurated by the Zahn brothers of Los Angeles. The mail was carried between Santa Catalina Island and Los Angeles by an unusual method of transport: carrier pigeons! An exchange of news between people on the island and the staff of the *Los Angeles Times* started with a column called "From Catalina." There even was a byline for homing pigeon "Clara."[3]

Meanwhile, in Europe, rigid airships soon replaced pigeons and balloons as mail couriers. The airships were not as finicky as the pigeons, and the weather did not affect airships as they did the balloons.

But zeppelin dirigibles were soon to take second place to a new type of aviation. In the early years of the twentieth century, the Wright brothers introduced the world to fixed-wing aircraft, which soon nudged out the zeppelins. Dirigibles made very stylish long-range flights around the world, but fixed-wing aircraft offered obvious advantages. They were inherently faster, less vulnerable to weather, and could go from point A to point B with more predictability.

In 1911, the first airplane air mail service in the United States started on Long Island, New York. For a week in September, Earle L. Ovington, in his Bleriot aircraft *Queen*, carried mail on a regular schedule from Nassau Boulevard on Long Island to Mineola, Long Island, New York, a distance of six miles. During that time, he carried 32,415 postcards, 3,993 letters, and 1,062 circulars. When he was over Mineola, he would drop mail pouches for the post-master to pick up.[4]

These early periods of air mail service later were given names. "Aero philatelists use the term 'Pioneer' to refer to flights of mail between 1911 and 1916. A later period, 1918 to 1926, would be termed the 'Government' period—the era when mail flights were conducted by the Post Office Department."[5] This distinction in nomenclature is important to stamp collectors and historians.

Pilot Bob Ellis had a rough landing near Rock Springs in the early 1920s in his de Havilland DH-4 mail plane. Icing was usually the problem. Keith Lambertsen

Right: A de Havilland DH-4 caught fire at Rawlins, Wyoming, on Thanksgiving Day, 1920. The unidentified pilot told rescuers to save the mail–not the plane. Keith Lambertsen

The aircraft of that period, however, were fairly primitive and underpowered. The de Havilland DH-4 aircraft was known as the "Flaming Coffin." A report on an accident on December 28, 1918, stated: "Lyman W. Doty, injured in accident at Belmont Park; plane No. 24238, DH-4, demolished; faulty axle; machine made of too soft wood; crumpled like an eggshell when the axle of the plane gave way; this pilot would not have been injured if pilot's seat had been located in rear where the mail chute is placed, instead of directly between the engine and gas tank."[6] Because of its location and poor construction, the fuel tank was a potentially lethal hazard. The landing gear was located too far aft and caused many embarrassing nose-overs. The weak construction of the fuselage resulted in crash fatalities. In some accidents, impalement and splintering resulted in serious if not fatal injuries. Nevertheless, in 1918, "though the air mail pilots flew through very bad weather at times, struggling against rain, fog, poor visibility, and heavy cloud formations, the record shows only one death for each 64,018 miles flown, and one minor injury for each 21,340 miles flown—in those days a record just short of fantastic."[7]

The air mail pilots were quite resourceful and would do anything to get the mail through. Once, in poor visibility, Frank Yager "on his regular run from Omaha to Cheyenne, ran into dense fog, landed and taxied [through fields] for thirty-five

Rawlins, Wyoming, was proud to have a durable hangar (right) in the early 1920s. It kept the pilots warm when the winds were strong. On left, is the warm-up hut used by pilots before the hangar was constructed.
Keith Lambertsen

Right: Air Mail pilot R. C. "Tex" Marshall, who was based in Omaha. Date unknown. Jesse Davidson Aviation Archives

Opposite: Air mail pilots and support personnel line up for a group portrait after the first air mail flight across the Sierras from San Francisco to Reno, Nevada, March 22, 1919. Nevada Historical Society

miles."[8] He added enough power to hop over fences whenever they blocked his way. Another time in Rawlins, Wyoming, when a local rushed up to help an unidentified pilot put out a fire that had just broken out on a DH-4 on the ground, the pilot yelled, "Don't worry about the plane! Just get the mail out!"[9]

The dedication of the pilots was expressed in the 1920 Postal Service's *Pilots' Directions:*

> Neither snow nor rain nor sleet
> Nor gloom of night stays these couriers
> From the swift completion of their appointed rounds.[10]

By the time it turned over its entire day and night operations to contract carriers in late 1927, the Air Mail Service had established the most articulated and highly efficient airway system the world had ever known. But the fledging years were fraught with dangers, tragic consequences, and death. In the line of duty, more than thirty airmen died while transporting the mail. But their sacrifices helped forge the aerial links that connected city to city, state to state, and ultimately, continent to continent. With their indomitable spirit, the pilots formed the backbone that brought about the development of a vast network of airlines that eventually led the world. In turn, commercial aviation has greatly affected our lives. Perhaps the overall sentiment was best expressed by R. C. "Tex" Marshall, a pilot in the Service from 1920 to 1927, in a letter to Jesse Davidson, dated January 4, 1953.

I think I have never been in an organization that had the esprit de corps that this outfit had. It's hard to understand how hard we tried to make a go of the air mail. The whole world seemed to be set on making us quit. Congress would not appropriate money. Newspapers constantly played up our accidents, and every man we met said it was just plain damn foolishness to try to fly the mail. But we knew it could be done. It wasn't the money. I came into the Air

Mail Service with my mind made up to fly not more than a few months to get the experience, but quickly found myself all bound up, life and soul in the experiment—for it was truly a great experiment. And we seemed so handicapped with only Otto Praeger [the second Assistant Postmaster] standing by us. The mistakes we made were honest mistakes. We were so wrapped up; we'd work hours that no one else would work on any other job. We just lived, ate, and slept our jobs. And how we did try. I know that in a few weeks after getting in the Mail, I was so bound up with the urge to make it work, I spent all my days at the airfield, all my time trying to help ... as did most of the others. The mechanics were loyal to a degree I have never seen since[,] working stretches of thirty to forty hours out in the cold and rain and snow without a word of complaint. It just makes me feel good all over that I was privileged to be one of the great bunch of men that showed it could be done.[11]

The Adams air mail pick-up system was employed by All American Aviation to provide air mail service to small communities in the east-central United States in the 1930s. Pilots, using Stinson SR-10F aircraft, executed drops and pick-ups at 100 mph. ©Museum of Flight

Robert W. Radoll had to be considered one of the senior air mail pilots in the early days. His license was signed by Orville Wright in 1900. Radoll flew mail between Chicago and Kansas City. ©Museum of Flight

This Seattle Air Mail Baseball Team of 1927-28 challenged the Seattle Indians. Claude V. O'Callaghan (eighth from left) was traffic manager for Varney Airlines and he had just thrown an Immelmann ball that had the spectators guessing. ©Museum of Flight

Above: Keith Lambertsen of Rawlins, Wyoming wearing an air mail pilot's uniform given to his father by famous air mail pilot H. A. Collison. His father, who took photos of the air mail pilots when they stopped for fuel in Rawlins, often did field repairs on the Liberty engines. Photo taken in February 2003. ©Bruce McAllister

Right: Varney Airlines pilot George Buck in front of a Varney Airlines Swallow biplane, displaying what pilots should carry when flying over uncharted territory. Franklin County Historical Society

CHAPTER 1
Aeroplane Station No. 1

The Aero Club of New York was busily engaged in making final preparations for a well-publicized ten-day aerial exhibition, scheduled to start on September 23, 1911, at Nassau Boulevard on Long Island. Despite the protests of peevish residents of the exclusive Garden City Estates and threats by the local sheriff, organizers locked in on that date.

The advance ticket sales indicated that the meet would be well attended. The public reaction was not surprising. Advertisements noted that prominent U.S. and European birdmen, some of whom were destined to become immortal in aviation, would perform daring aerial feats for large cash prizes.

But what would make this meet special was a simple gimmick—a memento that would keep the crowds coming out to the fair each day. Timothy L. Woodruff, a former lieutenant governor of New York State and president of the Aero Club, succeeded in interesting Postmaster General Frank H. Hitchcock in the idea of "aerial mail." Souvenir postcards and letters would be carried aloft each day and delivered to the postmaster at Mineola six miles away. There the cards and letters would be sorted and dispatched by regular channels to all parts of the country. In addition to the novelty, each piece of the first official aerial mail would, over time, become a collector's item.

Opposite: A rare photograph of Earle Ovington (second from the right) receiving directions for the first official U.S. air mail flight from Garden City to Mineola, Long Island, on September 23, 1911. Jesse Davidson Aviation Archives

The postmaster general sanctioned the delivery of aerial mail (and the cost) because the flights were an experiment and therefore did not require congressional approval. "William G. Sharp, an Ohio Democrat … argued that $50,000 for an aerial experiment did not seem excessive at a time when the government was paying the railroads $47,000,000 to carry mail. … he pointed out that Congress should support the development of aeronautics because the field held such enormous potential in terms of national defense, commercial advantage, and scientific research."[1] This latest form of transportation had been attracting attention. Two years before the meet, in 1909 the Army Signal Corps had bought its first airplane from the Wright brothers, and flights around Fort Myer, Virginia, by officers at the first military flying school there, created considerable interest in the commercial possibilities of air travel.

So the plan for the delivery of aerial mail was set. All mail collected from letter boxes on the grounds of the meet would be duly canceled and flown to its destination on schedule every day while the meet was in progress.

The opening date of the meet was set for a Saturday. Postmaster General Hitchcock notified Woodruff that he could not be present until the following Monday and asked for a postponement of the flight carrying the mail until then. Woodruff said that such a delay was inadvisable in view of the widespread publicity given to this aviation event. Deciding he could ill afford to miss this historic occasion to which he had given his official blessing, Hitchcock showed up on Saturday.

The opening day was lively and colorful. "Ladies carried fashionable Japanese parasols; many wore green and blue goggles. … a music band in red coats and caps played lively airs as 10,000 spectators filled the freshly painted bright green grandstand."[2] A large white canvas tent bearing the bold words U.S. MAIL AEROPLANE STATION NO. 1 across its roof attracted the attention of all who entered the grounds. A score of letterboxes labeled AERIAL U.S. MAIL were conveniently positioned on posts around the field. The novelty of the attraction caught the public's fancy just as Woodruff had predicted. Attendees formed long lines at substations to purchase stamps, envelopes, and specially printed souvenir postcards. Writing tables were located nearby. All day long, clanking lids of the collection boxes testified noisily to the popularity of Woodruff's scheme. Every half-hour, carriers made their rounds, scooped up the contents of the boxes, and brought them to the tent where each piece was hand canceled with the inscription "Aeroplane Station No. 1, Garden City Estates, New York, AERIAL SPECIAL DESPATCH."[3]

Everybody thought that the first mail flight would be flown by Captain Paul Beck in his Curtiss pusher biplane because he was the highest ranking military officer present. At scheduled take-off time, however, a troublesome engine forced Beck to cancel his flight. Those who might have taken Beck's place—Lieutenant Henry "Hap" Arnold (later to become chief of the Army Air Forces in World War II and other military pilots—were either aloft in their own planes or could not be reached in time to take Beck's place. Time was passing; Woodruff was in turmoil. The mail was in the bag, all 640 letters and 1,280 postcards! Who could carry the mail? More than an hour had passed and the mechanics were still fussing with Captain Beck's engine. Woodruff hurriedly tried to make an arrangement with some other pilots, but no one was quite prepared to carry any sort of cargo.

Woodruff looked around anxiously. Suddenly he caught sight of a cream-colored Bleriot monoplane glistening in the afternoon sun. Unlike other planes in which the pilot sat in the open between the wings, this one had a box-like body in which the pilot sat enclosed. Nearby, stood pilot Earle Ovington talking to his wife. Woodruff rushed over to him. "I'm looking for someone to carry the first letters dispatched by aeroplane," he said. Ovington, thoughtfully silent for a few moments, finally asked, "Is this the very first time it has ever been carried in America?" "The very first," Woodruff assured him. "I'll take it," replied Ovington. "Great! Let's hurry over to the mail tent and have you designated as the first aeroplane mail carrier in the United States," said Woodruff as he jubilantly linked arms with Ovington. Postmaster Hitchcock personally swore Ovington in as Air Mail Pilot No. 1. There was no time to lose, but they took just a few minutes for picture-taking ceremonies before Ovington climbed aboard his plane. Hitchcock handed him the bag containing the entire collection of the day. Now, almost two hours later than scheduled, a mechanic spun the propeller, the engine caught, and seconds later Ovington was racing down the field to his destination six miles away. Cheers broke loose from the crowds as the plane soared into the air. Postal officials breathed a great sigh of relief.

Lieutenant Colonel Henry "Hap" Arnold had barnstormed with air mail at country fairs in the early 1900s and was supportive of the air mail service. He helped fly some of the first air mail the very same week Earle Ovington did. Arnold went on to become the first five-star general in U.S. Air Force history. Jesse Davidson Aviation Archives

Above: Oath of office signed by Earle Ovington. Jesse Davidson Aviation Archives

Left: Earle Ovington (on right) poses with mail for first official U.S. air mail flight, September 23, 1911, at Garden City, New York. Jesse Davidson Aviation Archives

Frank Hitchcock (on left) hands the first official U.S. air mail to pilot Earle Ovington at Long Island, September 23, 1911. Jesse Davidson Aviation Archives

All through the meet, during which good weather fortunately prevailed, Earle Ovington carried the mail twice each day. On the third day of the meet, however, so much mail was gathered from the twenty mailboxes that the load had to be divided. Ovington flew one bag and Tom Sopwith, a contestant from England, flew the other in his Bleriot monoplane. On the fourth day of the meet, Postmaster General Hitchcock strapped himself in a seat beside Captain Beck in the Curtiss pusher and flew the route to Mineola with a portion of the day's collection, 62 letters and 1,400 postcards, dropping it to the waiting postmaster below. Upon his return from his first flight, an exhilarated Hitchcock was asked by a reporter for his views on the future of the aerial mail. He replied: "The usefulness of the aeroplane as a mail carrier will increase, but even in its present state it might be used to advantage over impassable stretches of country. The expensiveness of maintaining such a service is an obstacle, but that will diminish."[4]

Souvenir aerial mail was carried for short distances at other exhibitions held around the country during the remaining months of 1911. It always proved to be a major attraction.

Earle Ovington wrote of his unique experience as the first mail carrier soon after the meet

Earle Ovington flying the first official U.S. air mail between Mineola and Garden City, Long Island, on September 23, 1911. **Jesse Davidson Aviation Archives**

was over. After his death in 1936, his wife found a diary with his account among his personal papers. His comments reflect the thinking and cautious attitudes prevalent among the breed of airmen of that era:

> The aeroplane I used was my racing Bleriot monoplane driven by a 70-horsepower 7-cylinder Gnome engine. This engine is remarkable in many ways, but principally because the cylinders and crankcase revolve around a stationary crankshaft, while in the ordinary engine, the crankshaft rotates and the cylinders are stationary. The receiving station of this first aerial mail experiment was at Mineola. When all was ready and the mail securely tied in a bag and officially sealed, I instructed my mechanics to wheel out my giant monoplane *Dragonfly*. Those of you who have seen a monoplane in the air will appreciate the graceful outline of my machine, for the monoplane is truly a mechanical bird, while the biplane is merely a flying machine. When Bleriot made my monoplane he certainly didn't contemplate having it act as first aerial mail wagon for the United States Government, for he made no provision whatever for carrying mail or any other merchandise. When I got into my machine I found that the only space available for the purpose was directly in front of my control system. It would be necessary for me to place the bag on my lap in order to carry it all and be able to release it at the proper moment. As the bag weighed seventy-five pounds, you can imagine I had quite a bulky, though inanimate passenger. When I was ready, my chief mechanic gave the big propeller a spin and my Gnome engine roared reassuringly. Six men holding down the tail of my machine are necessary to prevent it leaving before I raise my hand as a signal to let go. When everything was working well, I gave the required signal and shot over the grass like an arrow from a bow. Gathering speed at every instant, I was soon going over fifty miles an hour though still on the ground. A slight pull of my elevator, however, and my aeroplane sailed majestically into the air and rose rapidly. Up I went, climbing the long invisible hill and steering in big spirals over the aviation field as you have seen a hawk spiral while watching its prey on the ground below. It was not until my altimeter showed me that I was 1,500 feet above the aerodrome that I straightened out my course for the Mineola field. You may wonder why I rose

Office of the Postmaster General
Washington, D.C.

September 30, 1911.

Mr. Earl L. Ovington,
    Care Postmaster,
        New York, N. Y.

Sir:

The following is a copy of an order issued this day:

"The postmaster at New York, N. Y., is hereby authorized to dispatch mails by way of Chicago, Illinois, to the post office at Los Angeles, California, one trip one way by aeroplane service (carrier Earl L. Ovington), provided such mails be carried by a sworn carrier, and without expence to the Department. Number the route 607001."

Respectfully,

Frank H. Hitchcock
Postmaster General.

to such a height to go such a short distance. I have always believed in high flying. It is not the fall in an aeroplane that inconveniences one, but the sudden stop. The higher you are the more chance you have to regain control of the machine before hitting the ground. And as hitting the ground usually means the finish of the aviator, this is a matter of great importance. Hence, I have always flown high. In this particular case I circled over the aerodrome so that if anything happened to my controls or engine I could land on the flying field with safety. On the other hand, from the height of 1,500 feet I had a good choice of landing places and so at that height it was safe for me to proceed to my destination. As I neared the Mineola field I noticed a man in the center waving a red flag. I judged this was the waiting postmaster. It would be extremely dangerous for me to attempt to land with a seventy-five-pound bag of mail upon my lap, for I was much restricted in the manipulation of my controls. The best thing to do, I decided, would be to work the bag of mail slowly over the edge of the machine with one hand while steering with the other and let it drop. As I came nearer to the field, I got the bag into such a position that only a slight push was necessary to start it overboard. Carefully gauging the position of the waiting postmaster and looking at my altimeter to get my height above the field, I calculated when I should release the bag of mail in order to make it fall as near as possible to the official waving the red flag.

At what I thought to be the proper instant, I pushed the burden overboard, and my aeroplane, relieved of this weight, bounded upward. I quickly turned to see the success of my aim and was gratified to find that the missile fell within fifty feet of the mark. As a matter of fact, this is a very difficult process, especially when the object

Post Office order given to Ovington to dispatch air mail to Chicago and Los Angeles, dated September 30, 1911. Note that under this agreement, the Post Office did not have to pay for this service. Jesse Davidson Aviation Archives

you are handling weighs seventy-five pounds and you have to steer the aeroplane and handle it with one hand. I couldn't throw such a heavy and unwieldy object; I just pushed it overboard and let gravity do the rest. In less than five minutes after delivering the mail I was back upon the Nassau Aerodrome. I had averaged better than a mile a minute. The fastest train could not have made the trip any quicker and an automobile would have taken four or five times as long. During the meet I had a talk with the Postmaster General and he seemed to be most enthusiastic about the future of the aeroplane with respect to the Post Office Department. He said there were many places out west which were almost inaccessible to the ordinary methods of land travel and he thought the aeroplane would be particularly useful under such circumstances as soon as it became practical. Personally, I am of the opinion that there is a brilliant future for the heavier-than-air flying machine in the transportation of mail and valuable express matter. And I'm glad the head of the United States Post Office Department is far-seeing enough to realize that, sooner or later, the aeroplane will be an important adjunct to the U.S. mail department.[5]

There was no doubt that Hitchcock saw more in this event than just another attraction at a fair. Later Hitchcock, in making up his estimate for Post Office appropriations for the coming year (1912), included an item of $50,000 for "experiments at carrying mail by aeroplane." "Even with the aeroplane as it is now," he wrote in supporting the request, "it will be useful to us particularly in some parts of the country. Take it along the Colorado River in the Canyon district of Arizona for instance, or in parts of Alaska. Along the Colorado River there are places where detours of fifty miles out of the way are made in mail routes to get to a bridge. An aeroplane could hop right across the river."[6] His request for funds was denied.

The following year another request was made urging Congress to appropriate money to launch an air mail service, The request was defeated again. It was clear that many opponents in Congress felt that Hitchcock was a bit too visionary for his time. At any rate, his fledgling mail carrier's wings would have to grow stronger. The aeroplane was still considered too fragile a machine to put to commercial use.

CHAPTER 2

Katherine Stinson: Air Mail Aviatrix

After a balloon ride in 1911, a determined twenty-year-old woman by the name of Katherine Stinson convinced her dubious father that if she became a barnstorming pilot, she might make enough money to go to Europe to study music and eventually become a piano teacher. At that time, barnstormers were able to earn as much as $1,000 a day.[1]

Pursuing her dream, in early 1912 she showed up for flying lessons at Kinloch Airfield near St. Louis, Missouri. The head of the school, Tom Benoist, was very leery of the young girl, but reluctantly allowed one of his instructors to take her up. At altitude, the instructor put the Benoist 12 aircraft into a steep bank, testing Katherine's airworthiness. Instead of frightening Stinson, he did just the opposite. Katherine was hooked on flying. Although Katherine was a natural pilot, Tom Benoist could not believe a one-hundred-pound girl could fly big planes, and he turned her down when she requested more lessons.

Katherine was not deterred. In May she found another school and an instructor who would show her the sky. The flight school owner and instructor, Max T. Liljestrand (who immediately told Katherine to call him Max Lillie), took to her at once and saw that she had the desire to succeed as a pilot. After only four hours and ten minutes of flight time, she was ready to solo. On her first solo, the engine on her Wright Model B aircraft quit after she had done a couple of figure eights and she expertly pulled off a dead stick landing. Three days

---

Opposite: Katherine Stinson with her Partridge-Keller Looper aircraft. Center for Southwest Research/Gen. Library/University of New Mexico/000-506-0053

Katherine Stinson was the fourth woman in the United States to get her pilot's license. She was also the first person in the U.S. to fly solo at night. Center for Southwest Research/Gen. Library/ University of New Mexico/000-506-0135

Opposite: Katherine Stinson at the Montana State Fair in 1913. Montana Historical Society, Helena

later she completed her flight test and became just the fourth woman air pilot in the United States.[2]

In 1913, Stinson appeared at the Montana State Fair in Helena, thrilling thousands of spectators as she arrived, piloting a "lettuce crate" (as those early aircraft were dubbed) across the valley and over the Continental Divide.[3] Stinson's Wright biplane, on display at the fairground racecourse, was the first aircraft many spectators had ever seen.[4]

At that fair, Stinson became the first woman pilot to carry the U.S. air mail. Before she would make any air mail flights, this dynamic aviatrix made a careful inspection of the interior of the fairground racecourse to determine it was suitable for takeoff. She was wary of the 3,874-foot elevation of Helena and the surrounding mountains. On the third day of the fair, Stinson took the mandatory oath of office "to support the Constitution and defend the mails." And defend them she did! When somebody asked her if she would take up passengers, she emphatically said, "No."[5]

On September 23, 24, 26, and 27, she carried pouches of mail from

the post office substation on the fairgrounds to the Federal Building in Helena. During the fair, Stinson carried more than 1,300 letters and postcards. She was to fly air mail on many other occasions—in Troy, Alabama, in 1914; in Seguin, Texas, in 1915; in Tucson, Arizona, in 1915; and for the Canadian government in 1918. In 1918, she set an endurance record of ten hours and ten minutes, flying the mail from Chicago to New York. The same year, she also became the first woman air mail pilot for the U.S. Post Office Department.[6]

In April 1913, she started the Stinson Aviation Company in Hot Springs, Arkansas, where her family lived at the time. It was obvious by now that Stinson was going to pursue aviation and not music. And her family also became very involved in aviation. In the next two years, her younger sister, Marjorie, and two younger brothers, Jack and Eddie, would take up flying and eventually become flight instructors. It is rumored that Katherine taught Marjorie to fly in two hours of ground school, using a mop and wash bucket as teaching aids to help Marjorie understand flight controls.[7] Of the two brothers, Eddie was more gifted at working on aircraft than flying them. He became a top-notch aircraft mechanic and went on to design aircraft that carried the Stinson name.

In June 1914, Katherine was the first pilot of either gender to fly solo at night in the United States. In 1915, in Los Angeles, California, she was also the first pilot to do night skywriting. With flares, she spelled out CAL.[8]

In 1916, Katherine and her family established the Stinson School of Flying in San Antonio, joining her old instructor, Max Lillie, who enjoyed the nice winter days in Texas compared to the harsh winter weather in Chicago. Lillie earlier had gained permission from the U.S. Army to use the military parade grounds as a flying field. Katherine's family was quite enterprising and managed the flight operations as well as doing aircraft maintenance. Her sister Marjorie became known as "The Flying Schoolmarm" and trained more than eighty pilots for service in World War I.[9]

But tragedy soon struck. Lillie "bought the farm" when his aircraft broke up in midflight. Undeterred, Stinson moved on from the tragedy, building her reputation as a top-flight stunt pilot and spokeswoman for aviation.

When the United States was drawn into Word War I, the U.S. Army twice turned down Katherine's requests to become a military pilot, even though the army was asking for volunteers. It was obvious that the army did not want women pilots; she was overqualified, if anything.

Opposite: At the 1913 Montana State Fair in Helena, Katherine Stinson used the interior of the racecourse for her takeoffs and landings in her Wright biplane. Montana Historical Society, Helena

Right: Katherine Stinson was the first woman pilot authorized to carry the U.S. air mail. In this photo she is picking up some mail in Tucson, Arizona, in late 1915. Center for Southwest Research/Gen. Library/University of New Mexico/000-506-0503

Determined to the end, Katherine joined the war effort by becoming a volunteer ambulance driver. Eventually, the harsh conditions and miserable European weather wore Katherine down, and by the time she came home, she had contracted tuberculosis. Her lengthy recuperation spelled the end of her flying career, but one of the world's greatest women pilots had worked her way into aviation history. Fittingly, upon her death on July 8, 1977, at the age of eighty-six, Katherine Stinson was buried in the National Cemetery in Santa Fe, New Mexico.[10] Although her brother Eddie designed the early Stinson aircraft, Katherine was the driving force behind building the family's name in the aviation community and in the history books. As of 2003, Stinson aircraft were still around.

Opposite: When she visited the Sioux tribe in Canada in 1916, Stinson was declared a "Princess of the Sioux" after she dazzled the tribe with a demonstration flight. By birth she was part Cherokee. The aircraft in the photo was her Partridge-Keller Looper. Center for Southwest Research/Gen. Library/University of New Mexico/000-506-0505

CHAPTER 3
Liftoff!

The importance of aircraft in the battles of World War I reinforced the view held by visionaries in the United States that airplanes had potential in many arenas, including carrying mail across the vast distances of the country. They also believed that air mail service could be a good training ground for pilots aspiring to military service.

The pressure for air mail service, which began in early 1918, was led by Assistant Postmaster Otto Praeger, a feisty Texan who had been a supporter of aviation from the start. Bowing to his relentless lobbying, the War Department finally agreed to jointly support a Washington–New York air mail route with stops in Philadelphia. According to the plan, the military would set up the Washington airfield, and the Post Office would set up the Philadelphia and New York landing fields.

The proposal was lambasted by its opponents as suicidal and harebrained. But Praeger ferociously took on and made short shrift of the opposition, as he hovered over the embryo of his hatching eaglet. The sky was the limit. There was even talk about experimenting with mail service in Alaska, but that would have been too ambitious,

Opposite: Major Reuben Fleet after his flight from Bustleton Field, Philadelphia, to Washington, D.C., on May 15, 1918. He ferried the aircraft there for the first air mail flight by Lieutenant Boyle. **Jesse Davidson Aviation Archives**

An aerial view of the U.S. Army airfield at the Polo Grounds (which later became known as the Potomac Field) in Washington, D.C., 1918. The arrow points to it—at 1,000 feet by 400 feet, with trees around the perimeter, there was not much room for pilot error, landing or taking off. Jesse Davidson Aviation Archives

Opposite: Although it was used on the first Army air mail flights in May of 1918, the Curtiss JN-4H Jenny was still used as a civilian air mail aircraft in the early 1920s. It was an advanced version of the standard Jennies that the U.S. Army used to train cadets for service in World War I. Jesse Davidson Aviation Archives

mainly because aircraft at the time did not have long-range fuel tanks or adequate payload.

However, when the United States entered the war in April 1917 and the War Department took control of aircraft production, the department would not spare any new-model aircraft for air mail service. The idea that air mail service would prove invaluable for giving military pilots experience in flying cross-country did not seem uppermost in some people's minds.

Nevertheless, Praeger quickly advertised same-day mail service between Washington and New York. He settled on Belmont Field, a racetrack on Long Island, as an ideal landing field in New York. The War Department panicked at the eleventh hour and became a reluctant bride. Only frantic negotiations kept everything on track. The army designated Major Reuben Fleet to run herd on the pilots and aircraft. He had only a couple of weeks to line up pilots and aircraft for the mission. Captain Benjamin Lipsner ran the administrative side of the operation. He also planned the first day's flights out of Washington (tentatively scheduled for May 15, 1918).

The aircraft of choice for this experimental mail run was the Curtiss JN-4H Jenny biplane, an upgrade from the Jennies used to train cadets. Ninety-five percent of all aircrew trained in the United States and Canada in World War I flew Jennies.[1] The JN-4H Jenny was powered by a

---

Previous page: A Curtiss JN-4H, piloted by Lieutenant George Boyle, ready to take off from Potomac Field, Washington, D.C., for Bustleton Field, Philadelphia on May 15, 1918. On this flight, he got totally lost and Major Fleet finally flew the mail north later that day. Jesse Davidson Aviation Archives

Opposite: On the first day of air mail service, May 15, 1918, Major Reuben Fleet, pilot, accepted mail for the return journey to Philadelphia after Lieutenant Boyle had gotten lost and never found his way to Philadelphia. Fleet ferried the first air mail aircraft to Potomac Field in Washington, arriving at 10:35 a.m. after making the trip from Bustleton Field in Philadelphia. He made the first leg in 1 hour and 55 minutes. Jesse Davidson Aviation Archives

150-horsepower Hispano-Suiza engine. Major Fleet ordered six Jennies from Curtiss Aeroplane & Motor Corporation and requested some upgrades. The forward pilot seat and controls were modified to accommodate the mail. Per Fleet's request, the fuel tank's capacity was doubled, as was the capacity of the oil reservoirs. All this was accomplished within two weeks.[2]

In setting up the world's first regularly scheduled air mail run, Fleet was facing a major logistical challenge: six aircraft did not constitute much of a fleet, especially if any had mechanical problems. On a daily schedule (except for Sundays), flights were to depart both Washington and New York at the same time with mail and fuel stops at Philadelphia. The postage-stamp size of the field on the banks of the Potomac River in Washington was going to challenge the pilots. It was only 1,000 feet long by 400 feet wide and was surrounded by tall trees.

A Curtiss JN-4H aircraft departing Belmont Field, New York, on the first U.S. air mail flight on May 15, 1918. The army pilots completed the flight to Washington, D.C., in three hours and twenty minutes. Jesse Davidson Aviation Archives

LIFTOFF! ▶ 39

On May 15, 1918, mail arriving by truck from Philadelphia to be loaded into a plane at Bustleton Field. Lieutenant James C. Edgerton then flew this air mail to Washington. Jesse Davidson Aviation Archives

Opposite: Lieutenant James Edgerton was one of the first air mail pilots and eventually was put in charge of Air Mail Service flight operations. Photo taken on January 8, 1919. Jesse Davidson Aviation Archives

On the inaugural day, May 15, 1918, Lieutenant James Edgerton was to fly the mail from Philadelphia to Washington. At 9:30 a.m. Reuben Fleet ferried a brand new Jenny to Potomac Field for the Washington outbound leg. The big brass present included President and Mrs. Woodrow Wilson, Assistant Secretary of the Navy Franklin D. Roosevelt, the postmaster general of Japan, and air mail service officials. Lieutenant George Boyle was to fly the first air mail out of Washington. As the attentive and expectant audience watched, the Jenny refused to start. Captain Lipsner thought that somebody should check the fuel tanks. They were dry! Finally, the problem was remedied, and Boyle took off. But his navigation skills left something to be desired. He headed in the wrong direction with the priceless mail, ran out of fuel, and landed on a remote field southwest of Washington. He had totally lost his bearings and ended up only twenty miles from his starting point.

The flights that originated in New York and Philadelphia were more successful, much to the relief of the air mail officials. At 2:50 p.m., Lieutenant Edgerton arrived at Potomac Field with 150 pounds of mail and copies of the *New York Times*.

The rescheduled northbound flights had much better luck than Boyle's abortive attempt and all made it to New York.

Years later, Reuben Fleet recalled (in Boyle's defense), "There were no maps of much value; they showed only political divisions with nothing of a physical nature except cities, towns, rivers, harbors, etc. … the magnetic compass was inaccurate and was affected by local metal on the plane and there were no compass bases to use in compensating each compass."[3]

After Boyle failed to navigate from Washington to Baltimore on a second cross-country check flight, Fleet decided enough was enough and sent him back to flight school. According to Donald Jackson, author of *Flying the Mail*, "Boyle's instructions were to keep the Chesapeake Bay on his right, a flight plan so faithfully followed that Boyle wound up several hours later at Cape Charles, Virginia, having flown a nearly 360-degree course around the bay."[4]

The press was more merciful to Boyle and did not dwell on his misfortunes. In fact, the *New York Herald* "proclaimed that nothing 'short of a hurricane' could stay these brave new couriers."[5]

LIFTOFF! ▶ 41

CHAPTER 4
From Khakis to Civies

Although the army pilots who flew the first flights for the U.S. Air Mail during the summer of 1918 often had trouble reading maps and staying on course, the Post Office reported that after two weeks of operations: "53 out of 60 flights had reached their destinations without unscheduled interruptions."[1] Relations, however, were not all that rosy between the army and the Post Office. The army did not want to waste its valuable pilots and aircraft, both of which were critical for the country's efforts in World War I. The Post Office, on the other hand, wanted daily and dependable air mail service.

Captain Benjamin Lipsner, the officer-in-charge of the Army Air Mail Service, was all for turning over the service to civilians. He knew that its future would be based on bigger, faster aircraft that could fly large quantities of mail over

---

Opposite: On June 6, 1918, Lieutenant Torrey Webb's Curtiss R-4 mail plane hit a pothole and upended on a field in the estate of the Boston Cabots at Saugus, Massachusetts. Bad weather and compass trouble forced the unplanned off-field landing. Jesse Davidson Aviation Archives

Above: Captain Benjamin Lipsner was appointed superintendent of the Air Mail Service on July 15, 1918. Date unknown. Jesse Davidson Aviation Archives

longer routes. Ultimately, military priorities and red tape were incompatible with flying the mail. And Second Assistant Postmaster Otto Praeger knew that Lipsner was the perfect choice to lead the new aerial mail service. On July 15, 1918, Otto Praeger issued the following press release: "In anticipation of the ultimate taking over of this service by the department, with its own equipment and personnel, Captain Lipsner has been appointed Superintendent of the Aerial Mail Service."[2]

The army closed out its part of the Air Mail Service in fine fashion in August 1918. Between May 15, 1918, and August 10, 1918, its pilots flew some 28,000 miles with only sixteen forced landings and no fatalities. Newly appointed Superintendent Lipsner wanted to keep this record going and sought out civilian flight instructors with at least 1,000 hours of flight time. They included Edward Langley, Ed Gardner, Maurice Newton, Max Miller, and Robert Shank. Lipsner also was on the roster as a pilot. Their salaries ranged from $3,600 to $5,000

Max Miller, one of the first pilots hired by Superintendent Lipsner, relaxing before a flight, 1919. He was killed September 1, 1920, when his aircraft caught on fire in flight. Jesse Davidson Aviation Archives

per year (depending on their experience), and they were given railroad passes so that they could go home on their days off.

At the time, Congress was facing large war debts and wondering about the feasibility of the Air Mail Service. Lipsner usually stuffed regular mail into the air mail sacks so that pilots would not despair about ridiculously light loads. There was not strong demand for air mail.

The civilian air mail service started with six air mail biplanes, which were purchased from the Standard Aircraft Corporation in Elizabeth, New Jersey. The planes were delivered on August 6, 1918. Named the Standard Jr. 1-B, the aircraft came equipped with tricycle gear that included a nose wheel. But the nose gear did not hold up very well and was soon discarded. Official U.S. Air Mail logos were painted on the sides of the aircraft. The

Harry Mingle (left), president of the Standard Aircraft Corporation, handing over delivery papers of six specially built airmail biplanes to Otto Praeger on August 6, 1918. Although these aircraft had the same 150-horsepower engine as the Jennies, they were faster and had greater range. **Jesse Davidson Aviation Archives**

FROM KHAKIS TO CIVIES 45

background for the logo was a crude drawing of a tobacco pouch.

Lipsner knew that a longer air mail run between Washington and New York was necessary to get more government financial backing. So he opted for a flight between Curtiss Field on Long Island in New York and Chicago, using his best two pilots, Max Miller and Eddie "Turk" Gardner. For the inaugural run, Miller would fly one of the new Standards, which had only a 150-horsepower Hisso engine, and Gardner would fly a Curtiss R-4 aircraft equipped with a 400-horsepower Liberty engine.

At 7:08 a.m. on September 5, 1918, Miller took off as planned and soon was flying blind through a heavy fog and dangerously close to the buildings of Newark. Gardner prepared to follow him, but before he could take off, the tail skid on his Curtiss R-4 aircraft broke. He rushed to replace the aircraft with another Curtiss—one that had just come out of the shop and not been flight-tested. Chief mechanic Eddie Radel came along on the flight to help if they had any problems with the untested aircraft.

Miller, meanwhile, was in the soup, with zero visibility and only his senses and his watch to navigate with. Several times he tried to get out of the fog and down on the deck. Could he trust his altimeter? Had he reached the Allegheny Mountains? Finally he broke out of the muck and saw the Susquehanna River below him. Quite low on fuel, he followed it to Lock Haven, Pennsylvania, where he landed, happy to be alive.

While his aircraft was being refueled, Miller made a short telephone call to Lipsner, reporting that he was in Lock Haven and that his Standard's radiator was leaking. After a pep talk from his boss and a quick radiator repair, Miller was soon airborne, fighting the rain and wondering if he could clear the mountains ahead. But lowering ceilings forced him to land. Suddenly, a farmer with a shotgun appeared and accosted him. "Git back in that machine and leave here … I know your kind. You're one of those fellers that sneak down on poor harmless folks just like hawks do on chickens."[3] Miller quickly took off, deciding it was safer to fight with the elements than put up with the locals.

Opposite: An aerial view of Curtiss Field, Long Island, New York. It later was known as Hazelhurst Field and then Roosevelt Field. Date unknown. Jesse Davidson Aviation Archives

Although Gardner made a valiant attempt to catch up with Miller, he failed because neither of them could fly at night. Miller's one-hour edge allowed him to slip into Grant Park, Chicago, at 7:05 p.m., just as darkness took over. Gardner and mechanic Eddie Radel made it to Chicago next morning, and the Post Office Department officials were quite happy with the results of this experiment. It boded well for future transcontinental air mail flights. But Post Office officials began to think the air mail could get through any weather, no matter how poor the visibility. Their attitude put excessive pressure on all in the Service. About two weeks after pilot Carl B. Smith became the first Air Mail Service fatality in a crash at Elizabeth, New Jersey, on December 16, 1918, Benjamin Lipsner resigned his post as general superintendent.

The early pilots, a proud bunch and quite independent, were also inclined to quit rather than put up with the pressure. On July 25, 1919, pilot

Above: Max Miller (left), turning over air mail to Captain Ben Lipsner after landing at Grant Park, Chicago, on September 6, 1918. Jesse Davidson Aviation Archives

Opposite: Ed C. Radel (left), mechanic, and Ed Gardner, pilot who flew in the early days of the civilian air mail service, and an unidentified man pose in front of a DH-4 in 1918. Jesse Davidson Aviation Archives

Leon Smith wrote a memorable letter to Otto Praeger, in which he explained his refusal to fly because of poor weather and inadequate equipment.

> I am writing you as my reasons why I did not fly the New York–Washington mail this morning and they are the following: The weather was very bad, there being a heavy rain, low clouds and not more than 200 feet visibility.
>
> You have through ignorance of the flying game placed on this route a machine known as the Curtiss-R with a very fast landing speed. In low visibility this machine is very dangerous as in case of a forced landing. The fields are so small that one cannot get down without crashing up. This was demonstrated only this morning … when Mr. Riddick, one of the flyers, crashed at Camp Meade. … It is mighty easy, Mr. Praeger, for you to sit in your swivel chair in Washington and tell flyers when they can fly. … Only yesterday

Right: Merrill K. Riddick, 1919. Jesse Davidson Aviation Archives

Opposite: Lieutenant Leon Smith (left) and Lieutenant John P. Richter in front of a DH-4B before an air mail flight. In 1919, Lieutenant Smith wrote a memorable letter, protesting management's indifference to pilot safety. Jesse Davidson Aviation Archives

FROM KHAKIS TO CIVIES 51

I flew through terrible rain storms with the result that when I got in here the paint was knocked off my wings and my propeller badly torn. … Pilots have been killed and only last week one of the best flyers in the United States lost his life when he tried to obey your orders and come through with the mail. Mr. Lamborn is the man I refer to. … I think, Mr. Praeger, that it is long past the time that a man with as little knowledge as you have of the flying game, Mr. Praeger, should be at the head of as large a proposition. … I did not refuse to fly this morning, but I did insist on flying a plane that I know was safe under the weather conditions, and you refused, nor would any other flyers take a chance.

Left: Charles Lamborn's aircraft crash site at Dix Run, Pennsylvania, July 19, 1919. Lamborn, en route from Bellefonte, Pennsylvania, to Cleveland, flew into some hills after he encountered fog. Four hundred and four pounds of mail were recovered. Jesse Davidson Aviation Archives

Right: Leon Smith (left) before a mail flight with Field Manager Harry W. Powers at Belmont Park, New York, May 15, 1919. Jesse Davidson Aviation Archives

May 15 - 1919
U.S. Mail Station
Belmont Park
N.Y.

With good luck
and best wishes always
H H Powers

It is true that Mr. Riddick got through after smashing one plane, but if one is lucky enough to do so, it is only by the grace of God that he gets through, and I assure you that he will not last long if he continues to fly in such weather with planes that are not suitable.[4]

Praeger had no choice but to fire Smith. Leon Smith's letter, which symbolized the air mail pilots' independence, helped stimulate improvements in aircraft, navigation, and certainly dialogue with management. Decades later, pilots formed their own unions to stand up to management. The perception was that nobody in management understood flying. Management also had its problems. Hazardous winter weather played havoc with air mail schedules and Congress wanted results, not excuses. Things would get better with time. Management had to learn to listen to pilots' needs.

Left and right: This modified de Havilland DH-10 bomber carried the first mail from Minneapolis to Chicago on November 7, 1920. Sitting on the fuselage are pilot E. Hamilton Lee (left), H. F. Smith, and L. H. Garrison. Standing are H. C. Starkey (left), W. L. Carroll, K.M. Stewart, and Burr H. Winslow. **Noel Allard Collection**

CHAPTER 5
Hell's Stretch: Surviving the Alleghenies

The air mail pilots long regarded the route over the Pennsylvania Allegheny Mountains as the most dangerous and unpredictable along the eastern seaboard. At the places that the air mail flights crossed east and west, low-hanging clouds if not fog often obscured the mountaintops. Pilots learned to question favorable forecasts and never take them for granted. The area became known as the "Aviator's Graveyard," and pilots who survived close calls shared their experiences with their colleagues. James D. Hill's story illustrates how resourceful those pioneer pilots had to be.

On an air mail flight in the mid-1920s, "JD," as he was known to his peers, lit up his usual cigar moments after he took off from Cleveland with mail destined for New York. The eastern terminus of the line at that time was Hadley Field at New Brunswick, New Jersey. His weather briefing included reports of low ceilings to the Ohio-Pennsylvania border, after which the weather was to improve.

Reaching Brookville, Pennsylvania, he climbed through the darkness, only to find himself in the soup. After climbing several more hundred feet, he could not break out of it, and he went on what meager instruments he had. As he bumped around in light turbulence, he glanced down to check his wristwatch and suddenly realized he had forgotten it. And to make matters worse, his panel-mounted clock had stopped.

Opposite: An aerial view near the banks of the Susquehanna River. The early morning fog often made navigation tough for the air mail pilots—especially before they had any navigational aids and compensating altimeters.
©William T. Douthitt/NGS Image Collection

Then he remembered the cigar. (He smoked the long stogies.) "Let's see now," he mused to himself. "I lit one up right after take-off from Cleveland. Cleveland to Mercer, Pennsylvania, is seventy-five miles. I flipped that butt out over Mercer. From Brookville to Hadley Field is another two hundred and fifty miles. So! Seventy-five into two hundred and fifty goes three and two-fifths. Simple. I smoke three whole cigars and two-fifths of a cigar."[1]

Always plentifully supplied with cigars, JD took out four from his breast pocket and placed them beside him. Settling down, he lit the first one and puffed away unconcerned as the de Havilland fought its way through the endless night. When he reached the butt end of the first cigar, he tossed it overboard and promptly lit the second; and in due time, that one was followed by the third and the fourth. When he was down to the estimated two-fifths, it went over the side too.

Hill throttled back and eased his way down through the fog in a long power glide. Finally, he broke out into the clear and soon caught sight of the rotating beacon with its welcoming intermittent alternating green-and-white flashes—Hadley Field at twelve o'clock (dead ahead). JD's hot clock had just become one of aviation's classic stories!

Pilots had to be resourceful on the ground too. In this account, which took place in Amish territory in Pennsylvania, Paul F. Collins, after battling the Allegheny elements (rain and fog) decided to make a precautionary landing when he found a hole in the soup. Breaking out at a safe altitude, he came upon an area dotted with neat farmhouses adjacent to long unplowed sections of land. As he landed, people appeared in small clusters at the edge of the field.

Their unorthodox apparel startled Collins. They wore long black coats and low-crowned derby hats with broad flat brims, according to their Amish tradition. Collins cautiously taxied his plane to a safe spot. The Amish milled about, conversing in hushed tones.

Quite soon, the threatening clouds broke up and the sun came out. Collins decided it was time

Opposite: Fifteen thousand people witnessed this first night air mail flight from Hadley Field, New Jersey, to Chicago in early July 1925. Postmaster General Harry S. New (left) is giving the mail to pilot J. D. Hill. Hill found a new way to navigate through bad weather. When he forgot to wear his watch on an air mail flight, he smoked a certain number of cigars to calculate his position. Jesse Davidson Aviation Archives

to move on. But how was he going to start his engine? The normal procedure called for a couple of strong-armed men—one to hold onto the prop and the other to hold onto the man holding the prop. At the pilot's signal, the twosome would give the prop a hard pull, and if they were lucky, the engine would start on the first or second try.

It was possible for the pilot to set the spark and attempt to start the engine by himself. But it was prudent to have someone seated at the controls, holding the stick all the way back, feet on the rudder pedals and left hand lightly resting on the throttle knob, ready to advance it slightly as the engine caught. Customarily, another person would place a pair of wheel chocks in front of the aircraft's landing gear to prevent the aircraft from lurching forward as the engine warmed up.

An aerial view of a typical stretch of the Alleghenies that air mail pilots had to fly over on a regular basis. Fog often obscured the mountaintops. The Alleghenies, sometimes referred to as "Hell's Stretch" and "Aviator's Graveyard," had the most unpredictable and constantly changing weather of the entire transcontinental air mail route. Date unknown. Jesse Davidson Aviation Archives

Collins scanned the poker-faced group and spotted a young man who looked smart enough to help him start the de Havilland aircraft. He briefed the young man in the simplest non-aeronautical terms on the task at hand. The Amish lad nodded understandingly and said, "Aye, so be it."[2]

Collins then boosted the lad into the cockpit and made sure that he had his right hand on the control stick and his left hand on the throttle. The trusting pilot then walked around the front of his aircraft, pulled the prop through its arc as gas hissed into the cylinders. Then he returned to the cockpit, set the magneto switches, again cautioning the youngster to "hold that stick all the way back." He cracked the throttle open slightly, placed the lad's hand on it and said, "Hold it right there. Don't move it."

"Aye," the lad replied.

Collins returned to the prop and was just about to pull it hard when he weakened with laughter at the sight of an Amish lad, with a big black hat, coat, and whiskers, in a most nonaeronautical role, sitting ramrod stiff. The assembled crowd did not think it was that funny.

Collins heaved the prop a few times without much luck. It was hard work, even for a six-footer like Collins. He went through the routine again when suddenly, BA—ROOOMMM! The engine fired, belching out a cloud of exhaust from its stacks.

He just managed to dodge the whirling blades and flatten himself on the ground as the wings passed over him. He had forgotten about chocks! Picking up speed, the big aircraft trundled down the field with Collins in hot pursuit. "Pull it toward you, pull it toward you," yelled Collins at the top of his lungs.

Frantically, the Amish youngster yanked at everything that moved inside the cockpit. An instant later, there was a blinding flash of light as a 50,000–candle power magnesium flare ignited, leaving a trail of fire and smoke swirling behind it.

Lloyd Bertaud. Date unknown. Jesse Davidson Aviation Archives

The unwitting pilot had tripped a parachute flare release. For a moment Collins thought his man was off on a short solo flight.

Still pushing and pulling at anything that moved, the lad providentially yanked the throttle closed and kicked the rudder pedals into a ground loop—the aircraft came to an abrupt halt at the edge of the field. Collins groped his way through the acrid smoke and helped the young man out of the cockpit.

The Amish lad looked skyward and calmly said, "The Lord directed me. I could not come to harm." Collins pumped his hand vigorously and assured him, "Mister, if that's the service you get from your religion, you ought to be an air mail pilot right away."[3]

Collins also had some other memorable flights during his days with the air mail service. On one occasion, Collins and fellow pilot Lloyd Bertaud shared the spotlight, but neither knew about it until they met a few days later and compared notes.

One cold clear night, Bertaud left Cleveland and struck out for Bellefonte, Pennsylvania, the midway stop for refueling and rest. From there he would continue on to Hadley Field. Soon after reaching his cruising altitude, he ran into unexpected murky weather and dropped to a lower zone so he could keep the light beacons in sight. Then he began to pick up ice particles and as he bore on, the ice clung to the leading edges and struts. He could feel the ship acting sluggishly, so he descended, hoping that warmer temperature would melt the ice. Although he didn't know it at that time, his friend Harry Chandler, flying in the opposite direction was picking up ice and finally cracked up in Wesley, Pennsylvania, but was not badly hurt.

At eight hundred feet Bert released a parachute flare. The flare contained highly combustible magnesium, which was packed in a metal canister to which a silk parachute was attached. Ignited, it burned with incandescent brightness for approximately four minutes as it descended. During this short time, the pilot had to get his wind direction, select the spot for landing, and touch down before the lights went out.

With little time to spare, Bert quickly set his ship down between the fences of a cow pasture and was just about to congratulate himself when the burning flare came down on the roof of a nearby barn. The barn, which was full of hay, went up in a blaze. Bert could see the door of the farmhouse fling wide open as the scantily dressed farmer dashed out in the cold. Bert dashed forward to help, pitching headlong over tree stumps and gopher holes.

"Save the stock, help me save the stock," yelled the excited farmer.

"I'll save 'em," Bert yelled right back. "Where are they?"[4]

The farmer's first thoughts were of his two husky Percheron draft horses. He led them from their stalls and tried to calm the terrified animals.

"The cows, the cows, get 'em outta the barn,"[5] the farmer yelled out of the darkness. Tracing the sound of the bellowing bovines, Bert raced to another part of the barn where he found ten Holsteins of matronly proportions groaning out of their lady-like wits. This midnight rumpus just was not in line with their normally tranquil dairy life. By the time Bert appraised the situation amid the noise of the cracking timbers, the herd was completely unstrung. He dashed into each stall, setting the cows free one by one and then, as if by signal, they stampeded out the door en masse, knocking him down and jumping over him.

"Talk about thundering herds," said Bert afterward. "Those cows did more harm to me than anything I've been up against in twelve years of flying."[6] But this was not the end of the episode.

By the sheerest coincidence, the very next night, Paul Collins was making good ground speed when bad weather forced him to make an emergency landing in the very same farmer's field at Mercer, Pennsylvania. Collins released a flare and landed. But the farmer whose barn had been burned the night before seemed surprised and relieved. "Good gosh, Almighty," he told Collins. "I thought sure you birds came back this time to get the house."[7]

Not all Allegheny trips ended so fortunately. In 1925, Charles Ames perished in a weather-related accident near Bellefonte, Pennsylvania. His accident was reminiscent of Lamborn's in 1919 (see Chapter 4). Ames, ex-barnstormer and army flight instructor, knew his way around, but the weather had deteriorated quickly and he lost his landmarks east

John McVeigh (left) handing mail to Charlie Ames at Hadley Field, New Jersey, in 1925. Jesse Davidson Aviation Archives

of Bellefonte in what had become known as "Hell's Stretch." When he failed to arrive in Bellefonte, an intensive search for him began, and the Post Office put up a $500 reward to accelerate the search for him. A fifteen-year-old boy finally found his body in rugged Hecla Gap.

Because of this tragedy, which pointed to the need for instrument-equipped aircraft, Howard Salisbury soon developed an adjustable barometric altimeter. Pilots henceforth could correct their altimeters as they flew their routes. Ground stations gave them corrected altimeter settings.

Opposite: Ame's aircraft wreckage. He was killed October 1, 1925, but wreckage was not found until October 11, 1925. **Jesse Davidson Aviation Archives**

Above, right: Telegram with news that Ames had been found dead six miles northeast of Bellefonte, Pennsylvania. **Jesse Davidson Aviation Archives**

Right: Reward poster that was printed after Ames disappeared. Search went on for over a week. **Jesse Davidson Aviation Archives**

Post Office Department
AIR MAIL SERVICE

OCT 11 1925

4 Q BX JA 86   BELLEFONTE PA.
SECOND ASSISTANT
WASHINGTON

SECOND ASSISTANT WASHINGTON A M S OMAHA ALL FIELDS PERIOD AMES FOUND DEAD IN HIS SHIP APPARENTLY FLEW INTO NITTANY MOUNTAIN AT HECLA GAP SIX MILES NORTHEAST OF BELLEFONTE AND ONE MILE EAST OF OUR BEACON LIGHT ON THAT MOUNTAIN WHICH IS THE FIRST LIGHT EAST OF BELLEFONTE THE MAIL HAS BEEN BROUGHT IN IT WAS NOT DAMAGED AND IS BEING FORWARDED TO CHICAGO PAUL AMES BROTHER OF CHARLEE NOW BEING FLOWN FROM CLARION TO BELLEFONTE HE WILL TAKE CARE OF REMAINS   133811

EGGE

REWARD $500

To the Person or Persons who FIND Pilot in Mail Plane Lost Thursday Night or Friday Morning.

NOTIFY Air Mail Field, Clarion, Pa.

In this DH-4 aircraft Howard Salisbury installed the first barometric compensated altimeter after the Ames crash in 1925. Finally, pilots could correct their altimeters to local settings as they carried the mail cross-country. Jesse Davidson Aviation Archives

Opposite: Band of brothers—pilots Rube Wagner (left), Wesley L. Smith, and C. Eugene Johnson worked for the Eastern Division, flying mail between New York and Cleveland. Jesse Davidson Aviation Archives

CHAPTER 6
Going West with Nutter

Between August 6, 1918, and its first anniversary, the Air Mail Service made a creditable showing in spite of severe winter weather conditions across the country. Skis were substituted for wheels, but they weren't very successful. Freezing weather played havoc with engine operation. Hot oil and boiling water had to be poured into engines to get them started. The Air Mail Service would try anything to keep the operation going.

During the spring of 1919, mail-carrying, path-finding flights along a seven-hundred-mile route from New York to Chicago were quietly carried out; the Air Mail Service wanted to prove everything worked before routes were established.

The de Havilland DH-4 was not too reliable. Overheated engines often caused premature landings, resulting in nose-overs and crumpled landing gear. Emergency fields became a top priority.

By the summer of 1919, air mail service was officially extended from New York to Chicago via Cleveland. The eight-hour schedule cut by two-thirds the best running time of the 20th Century Limited of the New York Central Railroad.

If weather conditions were fairly constant en route and with quick refueling and an exchange of pilots (at Bellefonte, Pennsylvania, and at Cleveland, and Bryan, Ohio), the eight-hour schedule was possible. But weather was always the big IF.

Opposite: Farr Nutter, date unknown. Jesse Davidson Aviation Archives

In October everyone was pushing hard to attain a record of one hundred percent on-time proficiency for this route.

One incident—one pilot, in fact—Farr Nutter made it possible. He was an unlikely hero in the making. He had separated from the army in January 1919 after a grand total of seventy-two hours solo—all in OX-5-powered Curtiss Jennies. He was not yet a seasoned pilot, but he yearned for a flying job. The army had turned him down as an air mail pilot, so he moved to Cleveland and found other employment.

One October day in 1919 he rode out to Woodland Hills Park and noticed a crowd milling about a de Havilland DH-4. It was ready to fly the mail, but its pilot was overdue from Washington, D.C. On a whim, Nutter approached the field manager, W. J. McCandless, and asked him why everyone was in a dither. McCandless explained that the Post Office Department required a record of one hundred days without default of any scheduled flights as proof that the service was practical, dependable, and should be supported by Congress. That day was the ninety-seventh; the next three days would be critical to attaining a perfect score and funds to extend the service to the West Coast.

By noon, the pilot still had not shown up and the situation looked critical. "The plane must take off by 1 p.m. in order to reach its destination before dark," said McCandless. "We fly only during daylight hours." At 12:15 p.m., one of the mechanics returned from downtown Cleveland where he had spent all morning checking the hotels for the missing pilot.

By 1 p.m., Nutter could not contain himself any longer and blurted out to McCandless, "I can fly that plane and I'm ready to go now if it will help you out." McCandless stared at Nutter in utter disbelief. "The colonel could not put you in that plane until you were checked out in Washington." Then as an afterthought, Mac agreed to take him to talk to Colonel John Jordan.

The colonel hardly acknowledged the two men as they entered his office. "Colonel, here is a boy who claims that he is an army-trained pilot and wants to fly the plane out right now if you will let him," McCandless announced.

Colonel Jordan took one quick look at Nutter and snapped: "He doesn't look like a pilot to me. Can you fly a DH plane?"

"I can fly anything with wings," Nutter snapped right back. (Nutter wondered what a pilot was supposed to look like. Maybe the old man was accustomed to seeing pilots in whipcord breeches, high-laced boots, floppy leather jackets, helmets, and goggles.)

Colonel Jordan gave him a menacing stare. "Do you have your army flight log?" he asked. Nutter gulped. "No, sir." There was another awkward pause. "Nothing doing," said the colonel bluntly. The interview was over. Nutter departed the office, deeply depressed, and joined a group of spectators milling about the pilot-less aircraft. At about 1:30 p.m., the colonel's secretary located Nutter and took him back to the office. The frustrated colonel stared at Nutter. "Damn it! Are you sure you can fly that aircraft?"

"Yes, sir!" With a tone of resignation, the old man told Mac, "Put him up. If he can't fly, let him take the consequences." As Mac and Nutter headed for the waiting plane, Jordan's secretary ran after them, "Please!" A few questions prolonged the interview. "Your name? Address? Next of kin? Who to notify … you know … just in case?"

Mechanics were standing by ready to pull the prop. By now, Mac was reading Nutter's mind and reminded him, "Pilots bring their own helmet and goggles." Nutter was in a light summer suit. He turned his cap around, put on a pair of sunglasses, and scampered into the strange-looking cockpit. As his eyes raced wildly about, a mechanic yelled out, "Switch off!"

The familiar hiss of the cylinders sucking in gas as the crew chief pulled the prop through a

Colonel John Jordan, superintendent, U.S. Air Mail Service, Western Division. Date unknown. Jesse Davidson Aviation Archives

couple of times sounded good to Nutter.

"Switch on!"

Nutter reached for the switch.

"On!" he shouted.

As two crew men held fast to the ends of the lower wings, the crew chief raised his left leg and prepared to pull the prop.

"Contact!"

"Contact!" Nutter sang out.

The prop spun downward. The engine caught and broke into a throbbing hum. Nutter cautiously ran up the engine, watching its vital signs and checking the magnetos. Mac rushed up to the aircraft and yelled out, "The colonel wants you to take off and land here before leaving the area." Nutter nodded in acknowledgment and signaled the crew to pull the chocks. As our hero advanced the throttle, the aircraft accelerated down the field. When the tail lifted, Nutter felt more confident. A slight pull on the stick, and the plane rose smoothly in the warm air.

At pattern altitude, Nutter gingerly banked to the left and leveled off. As he looked back at Woodland Hills Park, it seemed no larger than an average backyard! The last field he had flown from was a half-mile wide and a mile long. Well, that was Texas.

As he skirted the park, keeping his eye on the landing site, he suddenly decided, "The hell with it. Me land there? No, sir! Some other place, maybe. But not there. Not until I get better acquainted with this ship." Looking down, he could see small knots of people who looked like they were cheering him on.

In the rush to get the mail on its way, nobody had told Nutter where to go. It was either New York or Chicago. He decided in favor of Chicago. Maps. Where were the maps? Maybe he was sitting on them. He poked around the sides. Nothing. Well, that was that.

As he turned west, with the lower edge of Lake Erie on his right, Nutter wondered about the colonel. His orders had been ignored. He now had no plane. Nutter had not even taken the oath to protect the U.S. mail.

Nutter did know that he had 110 gallons of fuel—enough to take him to his destination. But nobody had told him about headwinds or that he could land at Bryan, Ohio (the midway point), if he needed more fuel.

Windy City, the next stop. It was a glorious day and Nutter took in the autumn landscape as the aircraft droned on. Soon Sandusky, Ohio, passed under his right wing and he spotted Toledo off to the north.

Nutter was unaware that the wind was pushing him south of his intended course as each minute passed. He should be seeing Lake Michigan soon, but it wasn't where it was supposed to be.

By now Chicago was still three hours away. The sun was getting lower and he had to find that lake—and soon. He retarded the throttle to conserve fuel. He began to see lights in houses and street lights go on.

Nutter decided he was off course. He turned north and climbed, hoping he could find that elusive lake. Within a few minutes he made out the glow of the great steel mills of Gary, Indiana, on the south end of the lake. After another few minutes, Lake Michigan revealed itself, and Nutter braced himself for the home stretch. His destination was still thirty minutes away. His fuel gauge was reading low. If the engine quit over the lake or city—well, he did not want to think of it.

He eased back the throttle and put the de Havilland into a long power glide. Soon a lighted office building in the Loop District grew more distinct through the haze. Within minutes he could see the lighted hangar at Grant Park, just a mile away. There was a sudden flash from the center of the field. Someone had ignited a small pool of gas to give him the wind direction. He braced himself for his first landing in nine months.

The fuel-starved aircraft settled fast in the cool evening air, and the whistling sound of the wings' brace wires softened as he leveled off on the home stretch. A hard thump and a couple of soft bounces signaled the end of the flight. Thirty feet short of an embankment, the aircraft came to a stop and within seconds quit cold—out of gas.

Minutes later, a tractor was towing the aircraft to the hangar as Nutter sat in the cockpit, dazed, elated, and exhausted. People were speaking to him, but Nutter could not hear a thing. Inside the hangar, the field manager rushed up to him and said, "Colonel Jordan has been burning up the wires about you and is waiting for word of your arrival. You'd better call him." Nutter suddenly realized that Chicago had been the right destination after all.

"No, sir, you call him," he replied. "He probably had a very unhappy afternoon because of me and I imagine he's not very happy now."

As the field manager wired the old man, Nutter escaped to a hotel, advising the manager where he could be reached. An hour later, the manager phoned Nutter and read him Colonel Jordan's reply.

CONGRATULATIONS. YOU HAVE A
PERMANENT JOB IN THE AIR MAIL
IF YOU WANT IT.

Nutter was too tired to sleep but finally he dropped off from sheer exhaustion. The next day he was back at the field at noon and the field manager advised him that he was on the schedule to do the mail run to Cleveland, departing at 12:30—in thirty minutes.

Soon Nutter was airborne and bucking headwinds. He blithely bypassed the Bryan fuel stop and hit Cleveland "on the nose." Without hesitation, Nutter made a perfect approach to the very field that had scared him the day before—and which had looked so small.

The colonel wasn't around but Nutter was advised to be at the field the next morning for a ceremony of sorts. He would be officially appointed as a full-fledged air mail pilot, with an annual salary of $2,250 (and eventually would receive pay raises up to a maximum salary of $3,600).

Farr Nutter continued to fly the air mail and the government never did ask him about his flying background again. He flew with the great air mail pilots, including Jack Knight and J. Walter Smith. And he was one of them himself.

To Farr Nutter, it was the best job in the world.

U.S. Steel's Blast Furnace No. 13 at Gary Indiana. In 1919, Farr Nutter used the lights from this plant to navigate by on his memorable flight to Chicago. ©U.S. Steel Corporation

CHAPTER 7
Memorable and Mortal Flights

Since the early days of aviation, most pilots have memorized the adage "Flying is hours and hours of boredom, broken by moments of sheer terror." Dean Smith, one of the great air mail pilots, recalled these important words in his book *By the Seat of My Pants*.[1] He also recalled that the mechanics and ground personnel believed that pilots "were a lazy and shiftless lot, lacking the gumption to get a real job and go to work."[2] In reality, air mail pilots in the 1920s did not have much training or the instruments for flying through bad weather. Often they had to play a guessing game with the Mother Nature and at the same time pray that their aircraft would stay in one piece.

Of all the early air mail aircraft in the 1920s, the most unpopular was the twin-DH-4; its only justification was that two engines were better than one. Its designers had downsized the 12-cylinder Liberty engine used in the DH-4 to two 6-cylinder engines. They did not realize that the weight of another engine and nacelle would handicap this "albatross of the air." The aircraft's take-off speed, cruising speed, and landing speed were almost identical. When General Billy Mitchell had once asked about using the twin-DH for his flight

---

Opposite: Before his fatal accident in early 1924, pilot Brooke Hyde-Pearson left a memorable letter for his fellow pilots–only to be opened upon his death. Jesse Davidson Aviation Archives

The twin-DH, built by Lowe, Willard & Fowler Company (LWF) of College Point, New York, was used by the air mail service between 1920 and 1921. Many called this design loose, wobbly and frail (LWF) and others said it was "a collection of spare parts flying in close formation." When General Billy Mitchell considered using this aircraft for his trip to the Far North, he was told that to fly the twin-DH to Alaska, he would need to dig tunnels first. Jesse Davidson Aviation Archives

Opposite: The twin-DH Model J-2 had two Hall-Scott engines, which had 150-200 horsepower each. The engines were also called Liberty Sixes because they used the same cylinders that the Liberty Twelve used. C. Eversole, who was the first air mail pilot to use a parachute, bailed out of a disabled twin-DH. This aircraft could barely maintain flight more than 1,500 feet above ground. Jesse Davidson Aviation Archives

to Alaska, he was warned, "In order to fly the twin-DH to Alaska, you'll need to dig tunnels first!"[3]

The twin-engine de Havillands were used on the New York–Washington route, and pilots in deliberate, controlled forced landings demolished a few of them. Some of these aircraft were also ferried to Chicago for use between that city and Minneapolis. Two fatal accidents took the lives of four men. One pilot bailed out when the prop on one engine split apart. Then there was only one of the weird-looking aircraft in service.

One day the sole remaining plane awaited a young pilot, Paul F. Collins, for the mail run from Minneapolis to Chicago. The ground crew made complimentary remarks about the ungainly bird. Collins had an inkling that they were being too complimentary.

"It's a great ship, Collins," someone volunteered. "How'd you like to take her up for a spin?"

"Naah, I don't want to trouble you boys. Thanks just the same."

"No. No trouble at all," they chorused in unison, "You really owe yourself the treat." The

---

Paul F. Collins checking freight before an air mail flight. Date unknown. Jesse Davidson Aviation Archives

ground crew went on to extol the virtues of the L.W.F. (loose, wobbly, and frail, as the ground crews described it among themselves).

Collins finally agreed to take it up after a careful preflight inspection. Soon he revved up each engine until each sounded right to him. This was the first twin-engine aircraft he had ever flown.

Collins took off, gradually climbing as he kept the airfield in sight. At 2,000 feet, he did some steep turns and figure eights. At 3,000 feet, he put the ungainly aircraft into stalls until it shuddered alarmingly. Then he coasted the twin back to the field, making a perfect landing. "A nice little ship," Collins commented as he climbed out of the cockpit. "Much obliged."

To his amazement, the ground crew turned their backs on him and walked in silence back to the hangars. Years later, at a get-together, one of the mechanics confided to Collins, " … the government would not let us scrap her. Then you came along. You looked innocent, so we wished her on you in hopes that you'd do us all a favor and crack it up. Of course, we hoped you'd do it without hurting yourself, but—well, when you brought it back in one piece, we just weren't interested in you anymore."[4]

Pilots often had to think fast and make repairs with whatever they happened to have on hand—or, as in this case, in a vest pocket. Elmer Leonhardt often flew low over the pleasant Ohio countryside when conditions were favorable, but for no particular reason this day, he was up to 4,000 feet riding along on a good tailwind, headed eastward, when suddenly, the control stick wobbled loosely in his hand. He wiggled the stick in all directions, but the aircraft would not respond. When he pulled back on the stick, it started to come out of its socket.

"Lennie" suddenly realized that the bolt that held the control stick into its socket had slipped out of place. As he attempted to push the control stick down into its socket, the aircraft started to dive. He ran both of his hands along the floor of the cockpit, desperately trying to find the missing bolt. Throttling back, Leonhardt bent forward as far as possible, patting his hand along the floor under the instrument panel. Suddenly, a small gold clip pencil dropped out of his vest pocket and rolled right into his outstretched hand. In a split second, he realized that he had a makeshift "fix," and he worked the control stick back into its socket, lining up the bolt holes. He then slipped the

Elmer Leonhardt. Date unknown. Jesse Davidson Aviation Archives

Opposite: Howard Brown before his untimely death in mail plane No. 318. Defective welding in its control stick joint caused the fatal accident. Jesse Davidson Aviation Archives

pencil into the bolt holes and looked for a safe place to land.

Luck was on his side that fateful day, and Lennie found a freshly plowed field. Rolling to a stop, he looked down at his repair; the pencil was in place but it had been crushed flat. In his report of the forced landing, he wrote that for want of a clevis pin, a pilot, his plane, and cargo might have been lost. He then added: "We ought to have the blamed clevis pins strengthened. I can't afford to waste a good gold pencil every trip."

In another more serious incident, Howard Brown was on a flight from Cleveland to Maywood, Chicago, bucking strong headwinds. As he worked the stick and rudder, trying to maintain level flight, suddenly, without warning, the stick flipped forward, putting his aircraft into a dive. By the time he figured out what had happened, his aircraft was too low for a bail-out and it crashed into a field and burst into flames. Badly injured, Brown crawled from the wreckage. Rescuers quickly found him.

At the hospital, he forced himself to describe exactly what had happened before he lapsed into unconsciousness. "Have those weldings fixed," he whispered with all the strength he still had, "or some more of the boys will get what I got." That night Brown died. Following his report, investigators finally determined that the upright tube into which the control stick fit had broken away from its horizontal counterpart. Reports from accidents like these eventually became what the Federal Aviation Administration now call "air worthiness directives" (ADs).

The grueling winter months of late 1923 and early 1924 brought with them some of the worst flying weather ever encountered along the mountainous region between northern Pennsylvania and Ohio. Pilots flying east and west over this range considered the route the most treacherous of the entire coast-to-coast system—even worse than the towering Rockies and the wild country below them, and farther west, the stretches of desolate areas.

Beaver Field, at Bellefonte, Pennsylvania, was the first scheduled stop west of New York. Nestled in the valley of the rolling country, the

Memorable and Mortal Flights

field was frequently shrouded with fog, which hid the surrounding higher terrain. Getting in and out of Bellefonte called for constant vigilance and adroit airmanship, weather conditions not always withstanding.

The trouble arose from the comparatively humid region of this eastern leg, where one could expect abrupt changes in temperature, dew point, and precipitation all within a matter of hours. It was not unusual for the mail pilot to take off under favorable conditions and run right smack into a swirling snowstorm less than twenty-five miles from the field. Attempts to turn back, as some pilots did, would often result in their being trapped in the valley below with but a slim chance of getting out at either end. A crash into the side of a mountain was also not unusual. And for a long time, there were more wrecks in those hills than any other section of the country. Of all the hairbreadth escapes, two tragic episodes stand out. They took place eighteen months apart—one under the worst conditions; the other, under fairly favorable conditions.

It was March 7, 1924. Brooke Hyde-Pearson took off from Bellefonte on a clear, cold day at 2:30 p.m. His destination was Cleveland. A short time later, a blinding snowstorm moving with express-train speed crossed his path at 3,000 feet. He pulled up sharply to get on top of it. At 4,000 feet, he was still in it, and the buffeting winds tossed his plane around violently. The compass made no sense, and the altimeter bounced up and down like a seesaw. He fought the controls to keep an even keel, for without a horizon, he could wind up in a constantly tightening spiral, inevitably resulting in a spin.

Late that afternoon, the family living on the Bloom Caldwell farm about three and one-half miles from Curwensville, Pennsylvania, heard, over the howling winds, the roar of a powerful engine as the plane raced overhead at almost treetop level. The noise seemed to fade away much too quickly as the ship went by, but they thought nothing of it.

At the dispatcher's office in Cleveland, the pendulum clock ticked off the evening hours. Hyde-Pearson was hours overdue. If the pilot had

---

Opposite: The Bellefonte, Pennsylvania, air mail field on a relatively nice day. The white circle, lower left center, is just above and to the left of the shop and hangar. Circa 1919. **Jesse Davidson Aviation Archives**

to make a forced landing, he would have notified either Cleveland or Bellefonte, whichever station was closest by telephone. By this time, both stations were making inquiries of each other. As night fell, so did the hopes of everyone at both ends of the line. Caretakers at emergency fields reported no signs of having seen or heard the plane during the daylight hours. Few members of the field crews went home to sleep that night.

The next day, between four and five o'clock in the afternoon, the children living on the farm, curious about the repeated trips of their little dog, Poodle, to the wooded gully below their house, decided to follow the animal. In a few minutes, they came across grizzly sight of Hyde-Pearson's crushed and partly burned body amid the scattered

The Brooke Hyde-Pearson crash site, March 7, 1924, near Curwensville, Pennsylvania. The renowned ex-Royal Air Force veteran had flown into a snowstorm on a mail run from Bellefonte, Pennsylvania, to Cleveland. He crashed into trees on top of a mountain and was killed. Jesse Davidson Aviation Archives

wreckage of plane parts and tree limbs snapped off by the impact. The snow that had fallen all night long and into the morning hours had almost obscured the scene from human eyes.

Bellefonte was notified, and a field crew hurried to the scene, arriving well after dark. In the glare of searchlights, they removed Hyde-Pearson's body and all the mail that could be salvaged. Then they made the long slow trek into town on the only conveyance available, a horse-drawn sled. Early next morning, the crew returned to the crash site and sifted through the wreckage. Already, some hardy souvenir hunters had disturbed the site. In the cold light of early morning, the crew saw what Pearson might have been looking for as darkness was closing in. To the north, less than one-quarter mile away from the point of impact, he would have had an open pasture to land in.

Pearson had been flying the mails for a little more than a year and, like most pilots, had had his share of close calls. He must have had a premonition of an early rendezvous with the grim reaper, for he jokingly remarked that if he had to go, it would be with his boots on—so he wouldn't hurt his foot when he finally kicked the bucket.

This tragic ending, which marked the career of one of the gentlemen of flying, also revealed a moving testimonial of his faith in the Air Mail Service. He left the following letter for his fellow pilots—to be opened only upon his death:

My Beloved Brother Pilots and Pals,
I go west, but with cheerful heart.
I hope what small sacrifice I have made
May be of some use to the cause.
When we fly we are fools, they say.
When we are dead weren't half-bad fellows.
But everyone in this wonderful aviation service
Is doing the world far more good than the public
can appreciate.
We risk our necks; we give our lives;
We perfect a service for the benefit of the world
at large.
They, mind you, are the ones who call us fools.
But stick to it, boys. I'm still very much with
you all.
See you all again.[5]

The letter was signed: Capt. Brooke Hyde-Pearson, USAMS.

CHAPTER 8
The First Transcontinental Flight

In 1920, as air mail service to Chicago from the East Coast became more predictable, the Post Office Department looked west to the next leg to developed: Chicago to Omaha. However, both those routes (like others that covered short distances) were not profitable. Longer routes and larger loads, the Air Mail Service reasoned, would ultimately be more profitable.

An experimental round-trip flight on January 8, 1920, between Chicago and Omaha went off without a hitch. In one year, the Air Mail Service had extended its routes more than halfway between New York and San Francisco.[1] As the routes extended west, the Air Mail Service arm-twisted towns and cities along the route to paint their names as well as compass arrows and quadrants on rooftops. The government was only too willing to supply the paint—and to play towns against each other to build airstrips.

As the routes expanded rapidly west in 1920, the accident rate went up with the additional flight hours. Pilot Dean Smith recalled:

In my earlier days I doubt if the number of completed trips averaged much over 50 per cent. There was hazard enough to suit the most avid

---

Opposite: The early air mail pilots saw this view looking north just west of Wendover, Utah. Pilot Peak, the snow-topped mountain upper right, was a good landmark for pilots to use. December 2002. ©Bruce McAllister

POST OFFICE DEPARTMENT

Office of Assistant Superintendent

AIR MAIL SERVICE

San Francisco, Calif.   November 22, 1929.

Postmaster: P E R S O N A L

WOULD YOU SAVE HUMAN LIFE ?

The Postmaster General has on several occasions requested postmasters to take up with civic and service clubs the matter of roof marking.

In my letter of February 18, 1929, you were informed that W. P. Fuller & Company, San Francisco paint manufacturers, thru the California State Chamber of Commerce offered to furnish your city with five gallons of paint free of charge providing a suitable location was secured and the paint applied. The offer of this free paint is still open, but we are informed that it will be withdrawn at the close of this year. Avail yourselves of this opportunity to obtain the paint free of charge.

This is your chance to contribute a real service to the advance of aeronautics. Not alone is it a pleasure to the aerial passengers to know by means of a painted roof the name of the town or city over which they are passing, but roof marking serves a greater purpose. It may save the lives of a pilot and passengers in case of fog or bad weather by identifying the city and indicating the direction and the distance to the nearest airport.

Accompanying this letter is a printed bulletin from the Daniel Guggenheim Fund for the Promotion of Aeronautics, which outlines and illustrates the best manner of marking roofs. Also attached is a questionnaire which you are requested to fill out and return to this office for forwarding to the Guggenheim Fund.

Please assist in this movement - Take the matter up with your Chamber of Commerce and the other live organizations of your community - Stay on the job until by persistent effort you have succeeded in having your city named from the air. Remember that as the dripping of water wears away the hardest stone so may constant and persistent efforts on your part wear away apathy and remove obstructions. As a man of power in your community get behind this roof-marking campaign and put it over. And, tell us what you did.

Respectfully,

A. O. Willoughby
Assistant Superintendent.

DANIEL GUGGENHEIM FUND
FOR THE
PROMOTION OF AERONAUTICS

BULLETIN ON THE MARKING OF ROOFS FOR THE PURPOSES OF AERIAL NAVIGATION.

The following information is designed to serve as a guide and aid in the marking of roofs by cities and towns for the purposes of aerial navigation. It is based upon the instructions issued by the Department of Commerce after research and experimentation with various types and methods of identification. Due to the fact that irregularity in marking may cause an actual hazard to the pilot instead of an aid, it is urgently requested that these instructions be followed as closely as possible. The smaller the town, the greater the need for adequate identification as the small town itself offers little means of identification from the air.

SELECTION OF ROOF FOR IDENTIFICATION

The selection of the building to be marked is largely a matter of local conditions and availability. The essential points to be considered are the ease with which the roof can be seen from the air and the location of the building. The roof selected should be on a building prominently situated. As pilots, especially when lost and seeking for bearings, follow railroad lines, buildings adjacent to railroad stations are often most desirable. The presence of large quantities of smoke, however, makes a building unsuitable as it reduces visibility. For this reason, buildings over which smoke hangs should be avoided.

Air marking on flat roof.

The railroad station in many cases lends itself ideally to roof marking. The Guggenheim Fund has requested the railroads of the United States to co-operate in this project to the extent of granting permission to use the roofs of their stations when the local group undertaking the work so requests. If there are two or more railroad lines entering the town, it is desirable to make identification near each. In any case, if more than one building is chosen for identification the value of the work is greatly increased.

The roof selected should preferably be of tile, shingle, tin or other metal, or of slate. Where gravel top or asphalt roofs offer the best location, wooden letters

NOTE 1. If the town or city has an airport, a smaller arrow in addition to the arrow pointing North may be added. This arrow should point to the airport and will be of much assistance to the pilot in locating the airport. If the airport arrow is used, the numeral designating the number of miles to the airport from the building should be placed above the shaft of the arrow. This is the conventional airport designation and makes it plain to the pilot that the arrow designates an airport and gives him the direction and distance. If the town or city has no airport, the sign should not indicate the nearest airport in an adjacent community as this would be confusing to the pilot.

may be elevated above the roof or the sign may be painted on a dull background formed of wood and raised on legs above the roof proper. Where raised letters alone are used, the gravel roof beneath should be treated so as to give a darker background than the natural gray of gravel. In most cases a suitable roof of wood, metal, or slate, will be found available and the name of the town painted directly on the roof.

Air markings on sloping roofs. If slope of roof is more than 30 degrees the name of the town should be painted on each side of roof.

SIZE AND COLOR OF SIGNS

A simple block letter in chrome yellow with a dull background, preferably black, should be used in all signs whether painted directly on the roof or not. White paint may be used instead of chrome yellow but the Department of Commerce prefers the use of chrome yellow as its visibility is slightly greater. The letters should be from ten to twenty feet in height and in no case less than six feet high. The smaller the town, the more difficult it is to read the name of the town from a safe altitude. A space of one-fourth the height of the letters should be used between the letters. The width of letters such as "M" and "W" should be two-thirds the height of the letter. Using the "M" and "W" as the standard for width, other letters should be proportionately less in width.

Where the roof is not large enough to paint the full name in letters of the proper size, a clear abbreviation of the name should be used rather than to reduce the size of the letters in order to use the full name. If the roof has a slope of more than 30 degrees the name of the town should be painted on each side of the roof.

Beside the name of the town or city, the marking should include an arrow of sufficient size to be easily seen and pointing due North with the letter "N" under or over the arrow shaft. This directional arrow is important as it makes it possible for the pilot to orient himself and determine his directions accurately.

The accompanying illustrations show graphically the manner in which roof markings should be made.

NOTE 2. If possible it is desirable that air markings be well illuminated so as to be easily readable at night. This may be accomplished by two or three small flood lights or by outlining the letters with electric bulbs. Neon lights also may be used effectively for this purpose. While lighting adds great value to the identification sign, the major immediate need is the identification of all towns and cities by roof markings. Further information on methods of lighting identification signs may be had from the Aeronautics Branch of the Department of Commerce.

Left and above: This letter encouraged towns to paint their names on rooftops to help pilots navigate to their airports—especially in bad weather. Doyle Werner

Opposite: This concrete compass marker, on a ridge east of the Rock Springs Airport in Wyoming, still is in remarkably good shape. It was used by the air mail pilots in the 1920s to crosscheck their headings and calibrate their compasses. ©Bruce McAllister

Above: Bob Burns, former mayor of Evanston, Wyoming, with a DH-4 wing strut from a DH-4 aircraft that crash-landed on Porcupine Peak, Wyoming, in December 1922. The DH-4 was piloted by Henry Boonstra, who survived the incident. ©Bruce McAllister

Left: Henry Boonstra. Date unknown. Between 1921 and 1927, he logged more than 3,200 hours of flight time for the Post Office Department–more than 303,000 miles. Jesse Davidson Aviation Archives

adventurer. Not all the forced landings were in fields; there were frequent crack-ups, some of them grim. The years 1920 and 1921 were the worst in the history of the Air Mail Service. In 1920 we had five fatal crashes, killing nine, a fatal crash for every 130,000 miles flown. In 1921 there were twelve fatal crashes, killing fifteen, with the average 104,000 miles flown per crash. As a pilot could expect to fly sixty or seventy thousand miles a year, his life expectancy would hardly make him welcome in an insurance office. I remember when Brooks Brothers refused to give me a charge account because my profession was too risky.[2]

Despite the danger and the losses, the Air Mail Service persevered in its efforts to provide coast-to-coast service. After "Buck" Hulfron completed a special trail-blazing 1,484-mile flight from Omaha to San Francisco on September 7, 1920, the stage was set for the inaugural New York to San

Randolph G. Page, 1921. Once he supposedly consumed approximately two bottles of whiskey on a mail run between Chicago and Omaha. On the plus side, he flew the New York-Chicago portion of the first transcontinental mail flight in 1920. Jesse Davidson Aviation Archives

William "Wild Bill" Hopson in a Curtiss R-4 air mail aircraft in 1920. It had a 400-horsepower Liberty engine. Between 1920 and 1927, he logged more than 4,000 flight hours for the Post Office Department—more than 413,000 miles. Jesse Davidson Aviation Archives

Opposite: Pilot John P. Woodward dropping off mail at Reno after a flight from Salt Lake City, September 11, 1920. Later that same year, his DH-4 aircraft, Air Mail plane No. 178, crashed into a hill in a snowstorm. Nevada Historical Society

Francisco air mail flight the next day. At 6:41 a.m. on September 8, 1920, Randolph Page took off from New York in his DH-4 with a load of about four hundred pounds of mail. Because "the mail load proved too great to fit into the forward mail compartment of the DH, Page ordered the extra letters placed into a suitcase that was strapped to the lower wing of the aircraft."[3] He was followed by William "Wild Bill" Hopson in a second de Havilland with a similar load of mail. Page and his relief pilots were to fly his mail by daylight hours only all the way to the West Coast, whereas Hopson's mail was to alternate between air and train, day and night.

Days later, Page's mail had a rough landing one hundred miles east of Reno at Lovelock, Nevada. Bad weather forced relief pilot John Woodward to make a precautionary landing there, slightly damaging the lead DH-4. Pilot Edison

---

Edison "Monte" Mouton, October 1922, at Elko Airport in Nevada. Between 1920 and 1927 he logged more than 3,800 hours flying the air mail. On September 11, 1920, he flew the final leg of the new coast-to-coast air mail service between Reno and San Francisco's Marina Field. **Northeastern Nevada Museum**

"Monte" Mouton, an ex–Lafayette Escadrille pilot who had just joined the Air Mail Service days earlier, flew the mail the next day to Marina Field in the city of the Golden Gate: San Francisco. He touched down at 2:20 p.m. on September 11, 1920.

Colonel John Jordan and the mayor of San Francisco welcomed Mouton. The first transcontinental mail flight had taken just thirty-four hours flight time (just over three days). Decades later, Captain Benjamin Lipsner, former superintendent of the Air Mail Service, noted that

> this aircraft had carried 16,000 letters and arrived in San Francisco 22 hours ahead of the best possible time by train, had the train made all [of] its connections. A saving of 22 hours in transit meant delivery on the West Coast two days ahead of schedule. The day this flight was completed was a very happy one for me, for at last the Air Mail Service had reached its majority. The baby I had nursed and pampered in its cradle days was now grown, and was proving itself a strapping, successful youth.[4]

The press was equally impressed. The *Literary Digest* proclaimed:

The mail fliers of 1920 are following the intrepid example of the couriers of Revolutionary times, the Pony Express riders, the frontier telegraph linesmen, and the railroad builders. Mrs. Alice Bartlett ... celebrated the Post Office's triumph in verse:

> *A rousing cheer from coast to coast resounds*
> *To you, swift couriers, controlling flight!*
> *Nor sun, nor rain, nor heat, nor gloom of night*
> *Shall stay you from completion of your rounds.*
> *To you! The big planes ride our skies each day—*
> *Transcontinental Air Mail: here to stay!*[5]

ALASKA'S MAIL SERVICE YESTERDAY AND TODAY
Aviator Eielson with Alaska's First Air Mail
Fairbanks-McGrath 380 miles
Feb 21st 1924

CHAPTER 9
Flying the Alaska Air Mail

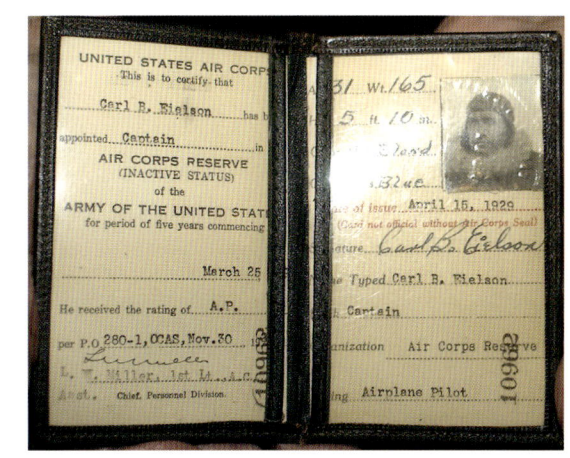

Ben Eielson's Air Corps Reserve identification card, dated April 15, 1929. ©Bruce McAllister

In July 1923, Carl Ben Eielson had the honor of being the first pilot to assemble and fly an aircraft in Alaska. It was a Curtiss JN-4D Jenny biplane and its home base was an uneven baseball field in Fairbanks. Eielson incorporated and named the enterprise the Farthest North Airplane Company. Its stockholders included newspaperman William F. "Wrong Font" Thompson and Dick Wood, the town banker.

Eielson's first cross-country flight was an aerial demonstration in Nenana, only an hour away from Fairbanks. After one hour of flying, Ben could spot only a solitary cabin, but not Nenana. The flat terrain and numerous rivers had mesmerized him. Luckily, he sighted railroad tracks, guessed the correct direction, and made it to Nenana. Eielson swore he'd never get lost again, and soon he was giving sightseeing rides, flying instruction, and hauling freight. He learned fast from his mistakes.

With plenty of mining near Fairbanks, he was soon in heavy demand for hauling everything from dynamite to food. His routes took him hundreds of miles to places like Nome, but the Jenny, with a range of one hundred and fifty miles, could not easily handle the long-range flights. So the next winter, he was off to the "lower 48," looking for a

---

Opposite: Ben Eielson piloted the first air mail flight from Fairbanks to McGrath, Alaska, on February 21, 1924. Eielson is in the foreground, just left of the cockpit of the DH-4 aircraft. Jesse Davidson Aviation Archives

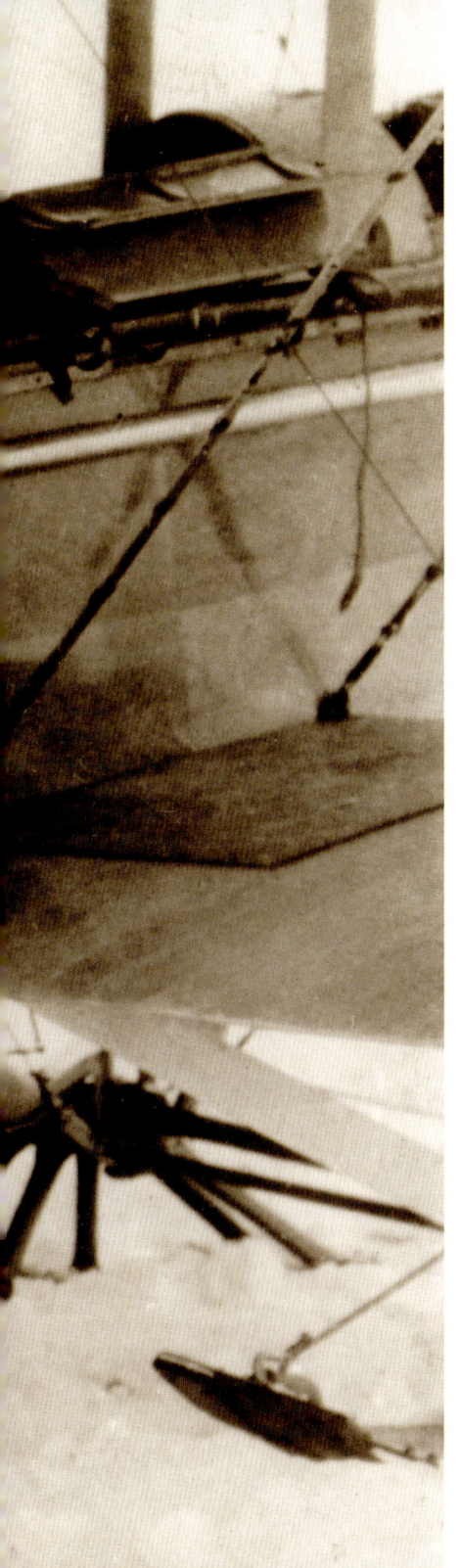

Opposite: Ben Eielson poses for a portrait before flying the first Alaska air mail, on February 21, 1924. 58-1026-740, VF Aviation Mail Service Archives, University of Alaska, Fairbanks

Town of McGrath, Alaska, in 1997. FAA

bigger "bird" and ended up in Washington, D.C., where news of his exploits had preceded him.

While he was in Washington, Eielson worked out a guaranteed mail contract with the U.S. Postal Service, and in early 1924, the Service shipped him a de Havilland DH-4BM aircraft with a 400-horsepower Liberty engine. It had four times the horsepower of the Jenny's OX-5 and twice the range. It came equipped with wheels, but Charles Schiek, a local carpenter, made a pair of skis for it.[1]

For this experiment, Eielson was to schedule two one-day flights per month between Fairbanks and McGrath—269 miles over mountains and wilderness. Under the terms of the contract, Eielson was paid $2 a mile. In contrast, moving the mail by dog sled cost more than $4 a mile and was subject to spring river breakup. Dog musher Fred Milligan had been delivering U.S. mail along the same route as Eielson for about twenty years; it took him twenty days to make the mail run to McGrath. Numerous times he saw Eielson passing overhead, "whistling like a spirit through the sky. … I decided then and there … that Alaska was no country for dogs."[2]

On February 21, 1924, Eielson departed Fairbanks' baseball field with one hundred sixty-four pounds of mail and plenty of survival gear. According to his later report to the Post Office, he had the following: "a full set of tools, a mountain sheep sleeping bag, ten days' provisions, five gallons of oil, snowshoes, a gun, an axe, and spare parts." His clothing included "two pairs of heavy woolen hose, a pair of caribou socks, a pair of moccasins reaching over the knees, a pair of heavy trousers of Hudson Bay duffle over that, a heavy shirt, a sweater, a marten ski cap, goggles, and over that a loose reindeer skin parka, which had a hood on it with wolverine skin around it."[3]

The temperature was five degrees below zero. In less than three hours he arrived at McGrath—a small interior community on the south banks of the Kuskokwim River; it served as a supply center for the nearby Ophir gold mining district. It took dog teams seventeen days to carry the mail the same distance. The trip had gone smoothly although neither his aircraft's compass nor its airspeed indicator worked.

After a brief lunch, at 2:35 p.m., Eielson loaded sixty-four pounds of mail for the return leg to Fairbanks. There were relatively few hours of daylight in February, so he knew it would be dark by the time he reached Fairbanks.

Opposite: The river country east of Fairbanks is similar to the terrain Eielson had trouble navigating in the winter twilight during his air mail runs. ©Bruce McAllister

Halfway through his return leg, Eielson had trouble navigating. What he was seeing did not match his map. By instinct and a good measure of luck, he eventually found his way back to Fairbanks in the dark. The townspeople had started a bonfire to guide him home. Unfortunately, he had to guess where the field began, and he hit a tree as he was landing. But he was not injured and the de Havilland would fly another day. The return leg had taken four hours and ten minutes.

Eielson made seven more trips to McGrath after the first one. But on subsequent trips he left Fairbanks earlier to have a better chance of making the round trip before nightfall. He also brought patients to Fairbanks on some of the flights.

Although Eielson had proven that air mail service was viable in Alaska, the postmaster canceled Eielson's mail contract after he had completed eight of the ten flights originally contracted for; the Service had made all-night air mail flights in the "lower

Opposite: Ben Eielson delivering air mail to Takotna, Alaska in 1924. Person on extreme left might be getting ready to start Eielson's de Havilland DH-4 aircraft. 68-69-619N, Lulu Fairbanks Collection, Archives, University of Alaska, Fairbanks

48" states its top priority. Although dog mushers grumbled and wondered what would happen to their business, as well as that of the roadhouses, an Alaskan wrote, "We are provincials … but a new trail is to be broken across the unfurrowed prairie of the northern sky."[4] Despite the cancellation, aviation had arrived in Alaska for good.

Eielson never gave up and was soon back in Washington, promoting air mail routes to places like China. Nobody took him seriously, but Billy Mitchell, as did Eielson, saw aviation as very important to Alaska's future. In late 1924, Eielson returned to the "lower 48," where he briefly studied law and also brushed up on his navigation skills and night flying in the Army Air Service. From 1926 until 1928, he flew about five hundred hours with famed explorer Sir Hubert George Wilkins on pioneering polar flights. On one of their most memorable record-setting flights, they flew nonstop from Point Barrow, Alaska, to Spitsbergen, Norway.

For his tremendous feats, President Herbert Hoover awarded Eielson the coveted Harmon

---

Ben Eielson in a candid moment—aircraft type not recognizable. Date unknown. Fran Christy Collection, 83-144-27, Archives, University of Alaska, Fairbanks

First airmail flight, Territory of Alaska
165lbs. of mail flown 280 miles in 2 hrs. 55 min.
Fairbanks to McGrath, February 21, 1924

Carl Ben Eielson

Farthest North Airplane Company DeHavilland DH-4BM

Trophy in 1929. But in late 1929, his great career came to sudden end when he disappeared and perished while trying to rescue personnel and furs off a stranded ice-bound schooner, the *Nanuk*, near the Siberian coast. Alaska had lost its first pioneer pilot. Many consider him the father of Alaskan aviation. Eielson Air Force Base in Fairbanks is named after him.

Visitors to Hatton, North Dakota, cannot miss the memories of Ben Eielson. An elaborate stone entrance to the town's graveyard is dedicated to him. The town's museum is in his original home.

Most of Hatton's eight hundred inhabitants are of Norwegian descent, as was Ben Eielson. From a young age, Ben learned the Norwegian work ethic. Like most boys, he showed an early

Commemorative Eielson air mail first day cover, signed by Noel Wien's two sons. Noel Wien was another famous Alaska pioneer pilot. **Pioneer Air Museum, Fairbanks**

FLYING THE ALASKA AIR MAIL

interest in things mechanical. His niece, Eileen Mork, curator of the Hatton-Eielson Museum in Hatton, recalls, "I remember that as a boy he showed an inclination toward aviation. Outside his home [which today is the Hatton-Eielson Museum], he often would sit on top of the windmill and pretend he was flying an airplane."[5] He also built a model flyer out of wooden crates and cloth. Essentially, it was a huge box kite and he would tie it to the top of the windmill, "fascinated by the sight of it soaring in one direction and then another."[6] Ben also was interested in the weather and kept a scrapbook of notable weather events, from heavy snowfalls to earthquakes.

Eileen Mork remembers her uncle's frequent visits home from Alaska. "He once brought me an ermine cape and always remembered to give me a special hug when he got off the train. He traveled so much that he never had time for girlfriends. He was fun. I am very proud of him."[7]

The museum has many photographs and documents from Ben Eielson's career—including

Eileen Mork, Ben Eielson's niece, in front of his childhood home in Hatton, North Dakota, June, 2003.
©Bruce McAllister

letters of commendation from Franklin D. Roosevelt and Calvin Coolidge. There is a prop from a Curtiss Jenny he flew in the Hatton area. But the centerpiece of the museum is the fuselage of the Fokker FVIIa aircraft *Alaskan* that he piloted for the Wilkins' Arctic expeditions from 1926 to 1928 and on the first nonstop flight from Fairbanks, Alaska, to Point Barrow, Alaska, on March 31, 1926.

The cockpit of the Fokker FVIIa aircraft, Alaskan, *which was piloted by Ben Eielson for the Wilkins' Arctic expeditions from 1926 to 1928. The entire fuselage is on display at the Hatton-Eielson Museum in Hatton, North Dakota.*
©Bruce McAllister

CHAPTER 10
Flying the Mail through the Night

Not content to continue transporting the mail by train at night, in 1921 the Air Mail Service decided to add night flights. On a twenty-four-hour-a-day schedule, the movement of air mail would make a great stride forward. But the timing was poor. The Service decided to commence night flights on February 22, 1921. Because of the weather and fewer hours of daylight, February traditionally was one of the toughest months to fly. To make matters worse, the aircraft of the Service were obsolete and had few instruments and radios. And the pilots did not have the luxury of lighted airways or emergency landing fields. Those innovations would come later.

On February 22, Elmer Leonhardt and Ernest Allison were to fly the mail west from New York and Harold Lewis and Farr Nutter were to fly the mail east from San Francisco. It was a long first night. Leonhardt was delayed by the weather west of Bellefonte, Pennsylvania. But Allison made it to Cleveland and transferred his mail to Wesley Smith's aircraft.

Flying from the west, out of San Francisco, Lewis "bought the farm" as his aircraft stalled on takeoff from Elko, Nevada. But Nutter cleared the Sierras (at 12,000 feet) and landed safely at Reno. Pilot Samuel Eaton then took over for Nutter the morning of the 22nd. He was unaware that Lewis

---

Opposite: Ralph Johnson ready for a night flight. Date and location unknown. Between 1924 and 1927 he logged almost 1,500 hours flight time for the air mail service. Jesse Davidson Aviation Archives

Above: A Sperry 36-inch beacon and landing light illuminate a crowd watching a DH-4 air mail plane that is just about to depart Omaha, Nebraska, March 22, 1924. Jesse Davidson Aviation Archives

James "Jimmy" P. Murray flew the Salt Lake to Cheyenne leg of the February 1921 experimental transcontinental night mail flights. Jesse Davidson Aviation Archives

Opposite: A DH-4 aircraft awaiting a night air mail run at North Platte, Nebraska. Date unknown. The de Havilland DH-4 was the workhorse of the Air Mail Service from 1919 until 1927. Often called the "Flaming Coffin," its reputation improved when the mail was moved to the forward compartment and the exhaust stacks lengthened. North Platte Airport Historical Society

had crashed just after they both took off from Elko, minutes apart. At noon Pilot James Murray took over the controls from Eaton and arrived in Cheyenne at 4:57 p.m., just twelve hours out of San Francisco.

As darkness approached, Frank Yager flew the next leg to North Platte, arriving at 7:50 p.m. This was the plane to watch! Jack Knight took over the mail for the flight to Omaha—the most dangerous one. There were few lights along the route and a broken layer of clouds at 2,000 feet. Along the route, farmers helped out by lighting bonfires to aid Knight. A second eastward-bound aircraft piloted by Harry Smith landed at Omaha before Knight, but Smith decided not to push on that night.

At 1:15 a.m. on February 23, Knight touched down at Omaha. He was to be spelled by

Harry C. Smith, June 1927. While Jack Knight pushed on to Chicago in bad weather on the famous night air mail run, February 22, 1921, Smith (in another eastbound aircraft on the same experimental air mail run) chose to stop in Omaha, Nebraska that fateful night, deferring to mother nature. Jesse Davidson Aviation Archives

Opposite: Jack Knight in a DH-4 mail plane. Date unknown. In February 1921, he flew the famous night air mail flight from North Platte to Chicago in adverse weather, proving that night air mail flights could work. Jesse Davidson Aviation Archives

an aircraft and pilot for the next leg to Chicago. But snow had grounded that aircraft in Chicago. Knight decided to push on and fly the second leg of four hundred thirty-five miles to Chicago. The future of the Air Mail Service was literally in Knight's hands.

With only a road map, he took off into the dark, windy night. Arriving in Des Moines, he decided to pass up a refueling stop because there was too much snow on the ground. At the next stop, Iowa City, he looked in vain for the bonfires that were supposed to lead him to the landing field. But the crews had gone to bed; they didn't think anyone was heading east that night. But an alert watchman heard Knight's plane and quickly guided him to the field with a red flare. As Knight touched down, his aircraft ran out of fuel. Things were going Knight's way that eventful night.

As soon as the watchman topped the DH-4's tank, Knight quickly took off into the Mississippi fog. Somehow he stayed awake and made it to Maywood Field in Chicago, landing at 8:40 a.m. Jack Knight had saved the Air Mail Service's reputation with his daring and resourceful flights. At Chicago it was necessary to cut his clothes loose to free him from the cockpit.[1] The moisture and freezing temperatures had frozen his clothing.

Jack Webster flew the next leg from Chicago to Cleveland. His trip was uneventful. From Cleveland, Allison flew the final lap to Hazelhurst Field, Long Island, New York. He landed at 4:50 p.m. on February 23—thirty-three hours and twenty-one minutes after the plane had lifted off from San Francisco. The age of night flying had arrived. The railroad, known as the iron road (or iron compass), would no longer be very important in the movement of mail.

But it would be some time before there were scheduled night flights. The Post Office Department still had to install radio beacons and improve night lighting at landing fields. And eventually, seventeen radio stations were also put in service. In 1921, the army experimented with the first lighted airway in Ohio between Dayton and

Right: A lighting catalogue from the 1930s. **North Platte Historical Society**

Opposite: Electric code beacons, such as this one in storage at North Platte, Nebraska, were situated every 30 miles along the air mail route in the 1920s and 1930s to keep pilots on course. ©Bruce McAllister

Flying the Mail through the Night

Above: The North Platte Airway radio station helped pilots stay on course into North Platte. Date unknown.
North Platte Airport Historical Society

Opposite: An air mail field service mechanic adjusting a 250,000-candlepower landing light on an unidentified air mail plane at Omaha, July 1, 1924. Jesse Davidson Aviation Archives

Columbus. Soon landing lights were put on some aircraft, and emergency landing fields were properly lighted. A consultant, Joe V. Magee, recalled how daunting the project was. "Col. Henderson was the big man in putting the airplane to work. He used to say that if the airplane was to be a practical mode of transportation, it must be flown at night." At Henderson's prompting, Magee started worked as a consultant on May 15, 1922, and lost no time visiting all the fields and talking with superintendents, field managers, pilots, and mechanics. He traveled by air in the DH-4s, sitting on a box in the mail pit. Because he was the first official from Washington to fly from coast to coast, as he put it:

> The boys took a liking to me. I also used to tote a generous supply of Scotch on my trips and that enhanced my popularity. We flew [discussed] airplanes long into the night in hotel rooms from coast to coast. And we talked [about] night flying many times until dawn.
>
> At first the pilots were quite skeptical about night flying. I didn't blame them. They had done a little—very little—during the war and they naturally took a dim view of the whole business.

One of the first things I did was to get the best brains in lighting … to get thinking about the lighting of the fields, runways, boundaries, obstacles and lights for the planes.

Experts at General Electric, Sperry, American Gas Accumulator and Pioneer Instrument, to name a few, got busy. … Col. Henderson arranged to have the Army install landing lights on an air mail plane … they did a good job in three weeks and it cost $4,500. We flew the plane back to Omaha and D. B. Colyer fitted up a dozen just like it. … we did experimental flying at North Platte because the country is nice and flat and in case we had to sit down at night, our chances were better there than at any other point. … [Henderson] was the prime mover. Never was there a man who paid less attention to red tape.

Left: Twenty-four-inch rotating beacons were critical to air mail pilots finding their night stops in 1920s and 1930s. ©Bruce McAllister

Opposite: Iowa City Airport, February 1925. Note landing light on de Havilland DH-4, which is about to depart or has just landed. State Historical Society of Iowa, Iowa City

Assistant Postmaster General Henderson (left), Radio Superintendent Edgerton, Chief of Air Mail Carl Egge, and E. Hamilton Lee, pilot, inspecting an improved 100-watt tube radio designed for use by the air mail pilots. The new radio had a range of 200 miles. April 16, 1922. Jesse Davidson Aviation Archives

Opposite: W. A. Strong, radio/telegraph operator on duty at Omaha Air Mail Station. Date unknown. Jesse Davidson Aviation Archives

A group of locals and pilots pose for a portrait at North Platte. They might have been celebrating a successful off-field landing. Date unknown. North Platte Airport Historical Society

Opposite: Landing fields in Chicago, Iowa City, Omaha, North Platte, and Cheyenne in the 1920s and 1930s, had floodlights (like the one on platform) with lenses that spread the light in a fan shape across the field for landing purposes. These floodlights gave pilots an almost daylight perspective on their approach. Nevada Historical Society

He ignored it. … In my humble opinion, Henderson was to commercial aviation what [Billy] Mitchell was to military flying.[2]

In August 1923, all was in place for test flights between New York and San Francisco. Things went very smoothly and the four-day test was extended to thirty days. Transcontinental air mail service was phased in by 1925, starting with New York to Chicago overnight service.

What we know today as night flying was slowly working its way into aviation. Navigation lights and flares were installed on seventeen Air Mail Service aircraft. Landing lights with 150,000 candlepower were also installed on these aircraft. At key landing fields, 36-inch high-intensity arc searchlights (with 500,000,000 candlepower) were installed. They could be seen as far away as one hundred fifty miles on a clear night. At these key refueling stops, large searchlights also aided pilots as they landed. Eighteen-inch rotating beacons were located at emergency fields, which were laid out roughly every thirty miles. By the end of 1924, lighted airways extended from New York to Salt Lake City. The Allegheny Mountains did not offer many sites for emergency fields, and beacons had to be located on mountaintops—not an easy task.

When complete, the lighted airway from New York to Salt Lake City stretched 2,045 miles and cost the Air Mail Service $542,000—a mere $265 per mile.

This DH-4 crash-landed in a tributary of the North Platte River. Date unknown. Before navigational aids were developed, weather or an engine problem was usually the cause of such mishaps. Louis Drost/North Platte Airport Historical Society

FLYING THE MAIL THROUGH THE NIGHT

CHAPTER 11
From Omaha to the Golden Gate

In 1920, the Air Mail Service set up its new western division with operations between Omaha and San Francisco. Colonel John Jordan was selected to run it. The division had fields in North Platte, Cheyenne, Laramie, Rawlins, Rock Springs, Salt Lake City, Elko, Reno, and Sacramento. There were emergency airstrips in between the fields.

The high altitude at which the pilots would fly would tax both the pilots and their machines. As Dean Smith noted, "From North Platte onwards the fields were much larger, a good thing, since our low-compression Liberty engines labored in the increasing altitude and demanded even longer runs for takeoff. ... [T]o cross the backbone of the Rockies we had to push the throttle clear to the corner."[1]

Flying west of Cheyenne, pilots encountered the rugged Medicine Bow and Laramie Mountains. But those ranges were just a warm-up to the 11,000-foot ridges of the Wasatch Range just northeast of Salt Lake City. Following railroad tracks, known as the iron compass, pilots then crossed barren country and deserts until encountering the challenging Ruby Mountains of east

Opposite: A freight train headed west between Cheyenne and Laramie, Wyoming, January 2003. The iron road was an easy trail for the air mail pilots to follow in the 1920s. ©Bruce McAllister

A recent aerial oblique view of Lee Bird Field at North Platte, Nebraska, emphasizes the wide-open expanses of Nebraska. Western Air Maps, Inc.

Opposite: Air Mail pilots had a government manual titled Pilots' Directions, *which gave detailed mileages between airstrips and descriptions of key landmarks as they flew across the United States. This aerial view is of Pine Bluff, Wyoming looking south. In the book it was described as follows: "The country between Sidney and Pine Bluff is the roughest on the whole course from Omaha to Cheyenne but plenty of emergency fields are found. A ridge extends southward from Pine Bluff, on which numerous dark green trees may be seen."*
©Bruce McAllister

Harold A. Collison piloting a DH-4B with air mail west of Cheyenne, Wyoming. Note grass caught on tail skid and trailing behind the DH-4. Date unknown. Jesse Davidson Aviation Archives

Opposite: A de Havilland DH-4 air mail plane flying over Sherman Hill, east of Laramie, Wyoming, in 1925. At the time this airway beacon light was the highest in the world at 8,600 feet above sea level. The airway beacon had 800,000 candlepower and was quite helpful to pilots at night and in poor weather. Jesse Davidson Aviation Archives

Nevada. If they had engine trouble or hit bad weather, the wide-open valleys provided plenty of emergency landing sites. By the time the aircraft encountered the Sierras, the pilots were well prepared to handle those relatively smooth granite-topped mountains for the final push into Sacramento and San Francisco.

The following quote captured the spirit of these pioneering mail flights:

> There's a speck in the sky and a drone
> on the wind,
> A sound as of harpstrings and drums.
> With its struts and its wires humming sweetly
> in tune,
> In the path of the eagles it comes.
> A man-made and marvelous bird of the air,
> The century's glory and boast,
> The plane, that through cloudland
> triumphantly bears
> Aerial mail to the coast.[2]

Some western refueling stops had specific problems related to altitude. At Reno, for example, higher density altitude made takeoffs very risky. (On hot days an aircraft at maximum takeoff weight would require a longer takeoff roll.) In addition, there were wires at one end of the field. Dean Smith recalled, "We used every inch of the field, pushing the planes back until their tails were against the fence. Leonhardt started first. He roared down the field, tail up to the very end, barely got in the air to clear the fence by an inch or two, and sank down on the other side. … [H]e flew on for another hundred yards before he could climb and disappeared into the distance, still dodging trees and hillocks. … I repeated Len's [Leonhardt] technique: I actually succeeded in clearing the fence. But on the other side I sank until I hit the far bank of the ditch, smashed the landing-gear struts up through the wings, nosed up and stopped."[3] Leonhardt and Smith were called to Washington for interrogation. It was obvious that the pilots were having trouble with their engines,

---

Opposite: This old air mail emergency airstrip near town of Medicine Bow, Wyoming, is still used by general aviation aircraft though it gets little maintenance and is not paved. ©Bruce McAllister

Earl Shobe, in his mid-nineties when this photo was taken, was a government radio operator in the 1930s in Buffalo Valley, Nevada, at an air mail emergency airstrip. In late 2002, he was still active as a ham radio operator. ©Bruce McAllister

Opposite: First air mail flight to Rawlins, Wyoming, in August 27, 1921, created the opportunity for a great group portrait of local dignitaries and their families. Keith Lambertsen

Air Mail to Rawlins — 1st Landing Strip & Hanger. Later Espys Golf Club & Course

Mail arrived Aug 27, 1921 at 11 a.m.

- ...lab.
- 13 Homer France
- 14 Fred Rendle
- 15 Perry Smith
- 16 J. P. Murry
- 17 Louis Schalf P.M.
- 18 Krebs
- 19 Ben Ashlock
- 20
- 21 L. C. Loren
- 22 Ive Earnes

Eddie Rickenbacker on a fuel stop at Rawlins, Wyoming, in early 1920s. Purpose of this flight in an air mail aircraft was unknown, but after the passage of the Air Mail Act of 1925, he started Florida Airways and landed some lucrative air mail contracts. That carrier eventually became Eastern Airlines. **Keith Lambertsen**

high altitude, and short landing fields. Washington finally agreed that high compression Liberty engines should replace the ones in use and that carburetors should have better mixture controls (to compensate for differences in altitude). It was also agreed that Reno airfield should be lengthened and that utility wires would be run underground off the end of the field.

The Air Mail Service now also acknowledged that different regions of the country required different pilot skills. "Flights over the Alleghenies and Sierras were to pay seven cents a mile, the Rockies six cents, and the Midwest five cents. Base pay was still related to length of service, but the top of $3,600 a year was soon reached. The new scale was hailed with delight by the pilots; it put us in the moneyed classes."[4]

The distances between towns and cities in the West also provided unusual challenges for the pilots. To better track air mail flights, the government started installing radios in air mail aircraft and developing land-based radio stations.

Earl Shobe, in his nineties in 2003, served as a radio operator for the U.S. Navy in the 1930s. The CAA (now FAA), which was desperately looking for

Captain Smith gets an assist after a Rawlins, Wyoming, fuel stop in early 1920s on the first U.S. Army 6,000-mile exploratory trip through the Northwest. Keith Lambertsen

East of White Mountain, Wyoming, Rock Springs airfield under construction in the 1920s. New Studio, Rock Springs/Sweetwater County Historical Museum

qualified radio operators, recruited him and other navy radio operators to man emergency landing fields for the air mail pilots and ultimately the airlines. At that time, radio was the only means of communication. Earl was sent to remote Buffalo Valley in the middle of nowhere in Nevada in 1937 and 1938. The nearest town was Battle Mountain. He used international Morse code to communicate with the master station at Elko, Nevada. "But we could talk with the airplanes by radio. The airway went from Salt Lake City to San Francisco. There were stations about every 50 miles along this airway. Master stations would take Morse code from the outlying stations."[5] Radio operators sent weather reports to master stations. From there, the reports would go out on teletype and then be rebroadcast by the big stations in Salt Lake City and San Francisco.

Earl remembered landmarks that pilots would use for their position reports. One pilot

This de Havilland DH-4 crashed into White Mountain after takeoff from Rock Springs airfield, due to severe downdrafts. Date unknown. Sweetwater County Historical Museum

Below: What appears to be a send-off party around an air mail plane at Reno, Nevada, in the 1930s. **Nevada Historical Society**

Opposite: The first three air mail planes to land in Elko, Nevada, in 1919 were surveying the air mail route. These U.S. Army de Havilland DH-4Bs had 400-horsepower Liberty engines. **Northeastern Nevada Museum**

likened a peak near Buffalo Valley to a feature of a well-endowed flight attendant's anatomy. There were more appropriate landmarks, however. In the vicinity of emergency airstrips, arrows pointing the way to the strip were painted on rooftops.

The station at Buffalo Valley had runway lights, a diesel generator, a building that housed the station manager and his family on one end, an office in the middle, and bachelor quarters on the other end. There were four shifts and the station manager would fill in if anyone got sick. For entertainment, Earl would usually shoot rattlesnakes. There was not much else to do there. Once he caught a rattlesnake and cooked it like a chicken. After his co-workers complimented him on the fine dinner, he asked them if they had ever eaten a chicken without legs. The joke was on them.

After his stint at Buffalo Valley, Earl worked at the Elko station for many years. After he left Elko station, Earl kept busy as a ham radio operator and communicated regularly with other hams around the world, including some in North Ireland,

Germany, Hawaii, and Australia. His wife gave him a distinctive handle—W7KOI—that stood for "Krazy Old Idiot."

The westward expansion of the Air Mail Service not only improved mail service but also stimulated the demand for better communications, more emergency airstrips, and aircraft with more power, payload, and range. In many cases, the radio and telegraph communications were superior to the telephone lines and gave the government an alternative communications system. These key innovations set the stage for contract air mail route and what would emerge as the nation's airlines.

The first de Havilland DH-4 to carry mail across the Sierras arrives at Reno, Nevada, March 22, 1919. Nevada Historical Society

Two DH-4 air mail planes at Elko. Date unknown. Northeastern Nevada Museum

An aerial closeup of Crissy Field, San Francisco, showing many army training biplanes and three larger unidentified single-engine U.S. Army aircraft. Circa 1930. San Francisco History Center/San Francisco Public Library

A 1930 aerial view of Crissy Field (upper center), the west terminus of the transcontinental air mail flights. The Golden Gate had not yet been built (see upper right). The Presidio Post is on the upper left and Fort Winfield Scott is at the top of the photo. U. S. Army Air Corps/San Francisco History Center/San Francisco Public Library

Above right: Postal employee showing off an early air mail poster. Date unknown. ©Museum of Flight

Opposite: Promoting the benefits of aviation, eight San Francisco women pose on what appears to be a U.S. Army biplane at Crissy Field, San Francisco, 1937. San Francisco History Center/San Francisco Public Library

CHAPTER 12
North America's First International Air Mail

The idea for the first North America international air mail flight originated in early 1919 in the mind of a most unlikely man—E. S. Knowlton, a prominent Canadian druggist in Vancouver, British Columbia. He was the director of the annual Vancouver Exhibition, which that year was displaying war trophies for the benefit of the Canadian Red Cross.

An imaginative promoter, Knowlton thought he might spice up the exhibition by inviting W. E. "Bill" Boeing (of Boeing aircraft manufacturing fame) to fly his seaplane up from Seattle and put on a dazzling aerial display over the city of Vancouver. Boeing warmed up to the idea and enlisted his test pilot, Eddie Hubbard, to accompany him and perform the actual flying display.

Bill Boeing had established an informal partnership with Conrad Westervelt, a naval officer, in 1915 and had built the *Bluebill* seaplane, known as the B&W. Later, this partnership evolved into Pacific Aero Products Company and eventually the Boeing Aircraft Company. He and Navy Lieutenant Westervelt hoped they could sell the seaplane to the U.S. Navy and other military customers around the world. But the Navy balked, so Boeing enlisted the

Opposite: Bill Boeing and Eddie Hubbard landing on Lake Union, Seattle, with the first North American international air mail, March 3, 1919. ©The Boeing Company/Museum of Flight

help of Tsu Wong, an aircraft designer, and developed what he and Westervelt hoped would be a more suitable aircraft for the military—a Model C training seaplane.

The U.S. Navy procured fifty and also ordered "one additional aircraft (A-4347) for test with a single main float installation and a Curtiss OXX-6 engine."[1] After World War I, the Navy declared the Model Cs war surplus and sold them for the original list price of $10,250 each. For the 1931 film *Dawn Patrol*, at least two of the planes were painted with German World War I markings and were purposefully crashed.[2]

On February 17, in Boeing's personal seaplane, Model CL-4S (a modified C-700; one of the fifty-one produced), Bill Boeing and Eddie Hubbard headed north from Lake Union, Seattle, with Anacortes, Washington, their refueling stop, en route to Vancouver, British Columbia. Large waves—always a threat to seaplanes—were breaking at the Anacortes harbor entrance, and while the seaplane was being refueled, the rudder controls broke. Luckily, Boeing's company had all the necessary parts available to repair the damage. On February 27, Boeing and Hubbard headed north a second time, only to run into wind and occasional snow. They wisely shut down at Anacortes overnight. The weather improved, and the next day was picture perfect. Without any further problems, they arrived on schedule at Coal Harbor, Stanley Park, Vancouver, in the afternoon.

During the next few days, Hubbard put on dramatic displays of aerobatics. Vancouverites had seen planes before, but not seaplanes doing loops and Immelmann turns, a maneuver in which an aircraft makes a half loop and then

---

Opposite: The original Boeing Airplane Company headquarters at Lake Union, Seattle. It was nicknamed the "red barn." June 8, 1917. ©The Boeing Company/Museum of Flight

Above: Front page of Vancouver Daily Sun, *March 4, 1919. Woman in photo at right, Mrs. J. Patterson, flew with Hubbard over Vancouver before the historic air mail flight.* ©Vancouver Daily Sun

NORTH AMERICA'S FIRST INTERNATIONAL AIR MAIL   155

Eddie Hubbard (left) and Bill Boeing stand near Boeing's CL-4S (a modified C-700) seaplane after arrival at Lake Union with the first bag of air mail from Canada to the United States in March 1919. ©Museum of History and Industry

resumes its normal level position by making a half roll. (It is used to gain altitude while turning to fly in the opposite direction) Hubbard also gave rides to key people in the community. His first passenger was Mrs. Jimmie Patterson, whom one Seattle newspaper described as "a game little society woman who came down after the flight smiling but awfully cold."[3]

Flush at the success of this aerial display, exhibition director Knowlton dreamed up yet another original idea. He suggested to his good friend Vancouver Postmaster R. G. "Bob" MacPherson that they give Boeing and Hubbard a sack of mail destined for Seattle. MacPherson agreed to the plan and no surcharge was added to what was the first international air mail to be carried between two countries in North America.

On March 3, with much ceremony, the first bag of air mail was handed to Boeing and Hubbard for the flight to Lake Union, Seattle, via Victoria (the capital of British Columbia). Victoria was a planned stop for Boeing because last-minute mail was to be delivered to and picked up from ships in its harbor twenty-four hours after they left Seattle.

For some unknown reason, on the flight south, Boeing and Hubbard bypassed Victoria, and the historic air mail flight took only two hours and ten minutes, with a fuel stop at Edmonds, Washington.

The air mail bag contained sixty letters, including one from Postmaster MacPherson to Seattle's Postmaster Edgar Battle. The letter read:

> Man made arbitrary lines may show upon the earth's surface, but when we mount up on wings as eagles no line of demarcation then shows between our young Dominion of Canada and her mighty ally to the south, the great United States of America. May the first air mail be the harbinger of thousands more to follow, so that our two countries may know more of each other.[4]

Bill Boeing concluded from the success of this historic flight that seaplanes of the future would be a viable way of carrying both air mail and passengers to such places as the territory of Alaska (and overseas). How right he was!

Above: This appears to be the Boeing 247 roll-out group photo, including Bill Boeing (in dark suit below nose of aircraft) and the team that worked on this project. The Boeing 247 was the first of many modern aircraft to be introduced in the early 1930s in a very competitive market. United Airlines bought the entire initial production of this model. ©Museum of Flight

Opposite: Seattle Postmaster Edgar Battle (right) handing Eddie Hubbard air mail to be flown from Seattle, Washington, to Victoria, British Columbia, on October 15, 1920. Hubbard eventually amassed over 350,000 air miles carrying the air mail between Victoria and Seattle. Pemco Webster & Stevens Collection/Museum of History & Industry

CHAPTER 13
Expanding the Contract Air Mail Routes

By 1926, after one year of operations, the contract air mail routes (CAM) had almost cut per-pound air mail handling costs in half. Representative M. Clyde Kelly of Pennsylvania proposed a significant amendment to The Kelly Act of 1925, which became law as H.R. 11841 on June 3, 1926. It read in part: "Existing contracts may be amended by the written consent of the contractor and the Postmaster General to provide for a fixed rate per pound."[1]

By setting a single air mail rate for letters, the Postal Service no longer had to calculate reimbursement to the carrier by looking at each letter; payment to the carriers was now based on the weight of the mail they carried. This streamlined the system so much that the amount of air mail flown increased from 3,000 pounds in 1926 to 473,102 pounds in 1927.[2]

In 1926 the postmaster chose to activate just five routes out of the seventeen applied for. They were:

CAM 1: Boston to New York via Hartford
Operator: Colonial Air Transport of Naugatuck, Connecticut
CAM 2: Chicago to St. Louis via Peoria and Springfield

Opposite: A J-4 Swallow aircraft piloted by Leon Cuddeback taking off from Pasco, Washington, April 6, 1926, on the inaugural air mail flight to Elko. There were 2,500 spectators present. **Northeastern Nevada Museum**

A stagecoach delivered mail to the first Pasco to Boise to Elko air mail flight in 1926. Franklin County Historical Society

Opposite: Leon Cuddeback, pilot of first air mail flight from Pasco, Washington, to Elko, Nevada, April 6, 1926. This open-cockpit J-4 Swallow biplane was the pride of Varney Airlines and featured a 200-horsepower air-cooled Wright Whirlwind engine. Boise was a mail stop on this new route. Northeastern Nevada Museum

Operator: Robertson Aircraft Corporation of St. Louis, Missouri

CAM 3: Chicago to Dallas and Ft. Worth

Operator: National Air Transport of Chicago, Illinois

CAM 4: Salt Lake City to Los Angeles

Operator: Western Air Express of Los Angeles, California

CAM 5: Elko, Nevada, to Pasco, Washington

Operator: Walter Varney of San Francisco, California

CAM 5 Route between Elko, Nevada, and Pasco, Washington, was one of the more unusual routes. Few bidders were interested in this challenging route because it went through rugged and remote country. Billy Mitchell commented, "If they knew what they were trying to do, they wouldn't even start it."[3] But Walter Varney was equal to the challenge, made the winning bid, and decided to use some modified Swallow aircraft with a redesigned wing and 150-horsepower Curtiss K-6 engines for the route. He also drove the route in his

Above: The CAM 5 dispatch form used on April 6, 1926. Pilot Cuddeback flew one bag of air mail from Pasco, Washington, to Elko, Nevada. Franklin County Historical Society

Opposite: *Leon Cuddeback in front of a United Airlines jet and a rebuilt Swallow at Pasco airport at the fiftieth anniversary celebration on April 6, 1976, commemorating the first Pasco air mail flight.*
Ralph Smith/Franklin County Historical Society

Above: The rugged Blue Mountains between Boise, Idaho, and Pasco, Washington, challenged the air mail pilots. After surviving a crash-landing, one pilot hiked out. It was months before his mail was found. Only one letter was recovered. Franklin County Historical Society

Air mail pilot Walter Cuse (left) and fellow unidentified pilot display pistols they had to carry to defend their air mail. Date unknown. Franklin County Historical Society

car and drew up maps for his pilots. His maps included highways, railroad tracks, and in some cases, even dirt roads.

The inaugural flight was almost delayed when two ferry pilots damaged Varney's Swallows while landing at Pasco the day before the inaugural flight. On top of that, both of the pilots broke their noses. Leon Cuddeback flew the inaugural mail, with a big sendoff from Pasco. Cowboys on a stagecoach handed him the first six sacks of mail. The press came from the West Coast and Spokane to cover the historic event. His flight to Elko was uneventful but a thunderstorm forced him to follow the roads part of the 244-mile flight. Pilot Franklin Rose flew the return leg and had a rougher time. He was blown way off-course by the very same thunderstorm Cuddeback had avoided, and he eventually had to make a precautionary landing in Jordan Valley, Oregon. But Rose was a resourceful pilot and hiked about ten miles with his mail to a farm. The surprised farmer loaned him a horse, and he rode another thirty miles to a telephone. It took two more days for the mail to make it to its intended destination—Pasco, Washington.

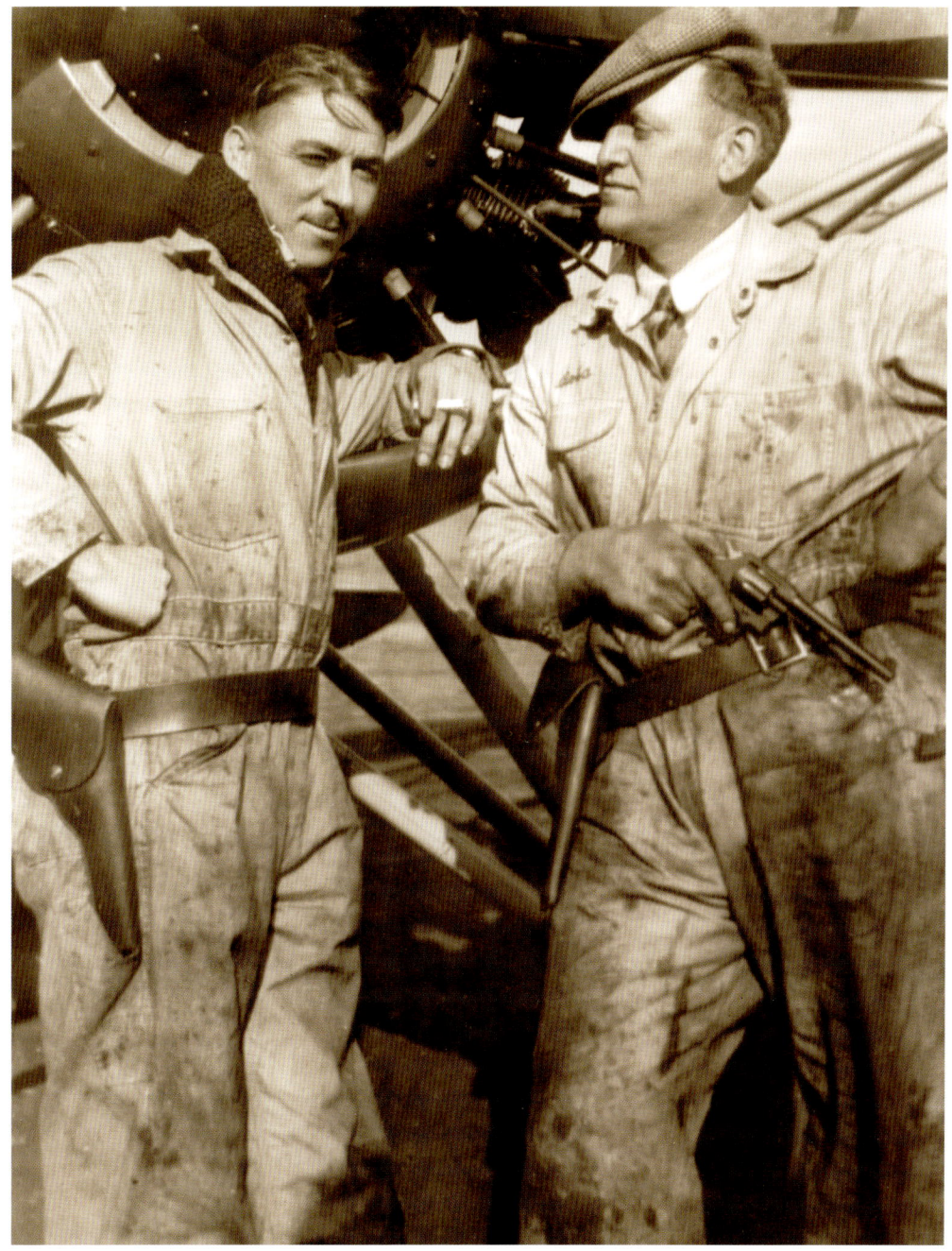

Opposite: This 1926 air mail route map shows the difference in moving the air mail by aircraft versus trains. Franklin County Historical Society

Right: Portrait of Walter Varney, date unknown. His airline won the Elko, Nevada, to Pasco, Washington, CAM route on October 7, 1925. ©Museum of Flight

A Varney Airlines radio position map illustrates the complex logistics of CAM route operations. ©Museum of Flight

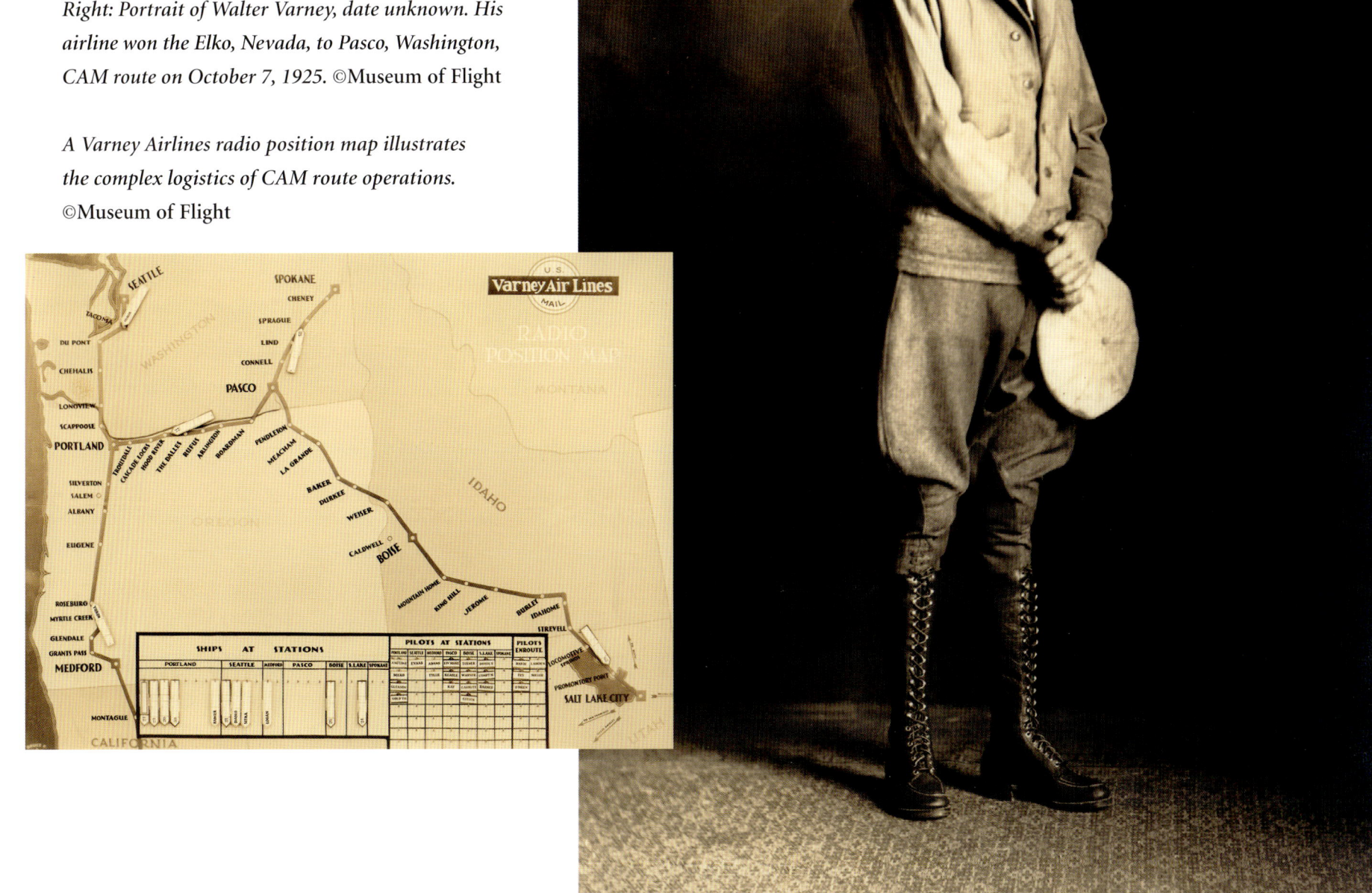

Rural post office near Salt Lake City. Date unknown. Special Collections, J. W. Marriott Library, University of Utah

Opposite: On April 17, 1926, Jimmy James flew the inaugural air mail flight from Salt Lake City to Los Angeles.
Special Collections, J. W. Marriott Library, University of Utah

The air mail loads were getting too heavy for the de Havilland DH-4s, which were beginning to show their age. The Douglas Aircraft Company came to the rescue with its M-4 aircraft. It could carry 1,000 pounds of mail and cruise as high as 17,500 feet, which was essential for getting on top of bad weather and clearing the Rockies with room to spare. With its greater range, the M-4 could bypass some previously important fuel stops like Rawlins, Wyoming, Bryan, Ohio, and Bellefonte, Pennsylvania. These stops were gradually phased out and other fuel stops (North Platte, Nebraska, and Iowa City, Iowa) were no longer required fuel stops for eastbound flights.

The Douglas M-4 aircraft was used for all flights east of Salt Lake City. Douglas M-2s and DH-4s continued to carry the mail from Salt Lake City to the West Coast. Eventually, the government phased out the DH-4s and sold the M-4s to the contract air mail carriers—most of which went on to become the country's biggest airlines.

In the late 1920s, Varney Airlines used Boeing 40-B2 aircraft to fly air mail to and from Salt Lake City. The later models had 525-horsepower engines and could carry 1,500 pounds of mail and four passengers in a tiny noisy cabin.
Special Collections, J. W. Marriott Library, University of Utah

Opposite: Loading the air mail on a Douglas M-2 mail plane in 1926 in Salt Lake City for a flight to Los Angeles. The reliable 400-horsepower Liberty engine enabled this aircraft to cruise at 120 mph with 1,000 pounds of mail.
Special Collections, J. W. Marriott Library, University of Utah

CHAPTER 14
The Airlines Are Born

As early as 1925, large corporations, such as the Ford Motor Company, saw the tremendous profit potential in the air transport business and became interested in it. In April of that year, Ford started daily flights between Chicago and Dearborn, Michigan. By the end of the year, Cleveland, Ohio, was included and the frequency of the flights increased. Ford had what amounted to the first airline in the United States. Although the airline did not serve the general public, it was the first carrier to fly freight and passengers (it flew its personnel on the air mail runs).

At first, Ford's aircraft of choice was the Stout 2-AT equipped with a 400-horsepower Liberty engine. Ford eventually bought out Stout and tried to make the 2-AT into a trimotored aircraft. That project failed, but Ford engineers stuck with the three-engine concept and came out with what became known as the "Tin Goose"—the Ford Trimotor.

At the same time, the Air Mail Service was looking at radio technology for both communications and navigation. Good navigation equipment would be vital to the airlines in the future—especially for flights in bad weather and at night. In

---

Opposite: A Ford 5-AT-C Trimotor NC-8419 at the terminal, St. Paul Airport, circa 1932. This historic building was demolished in 1988 to make space for a new runway approach at Holman Field. **Northwest Airlines/Noel Allard Collection**

January 1925, Carl Egge, superintendent of the Air Mail Service, asked for and received permission to establish an "experimental laboratory" to test radio direction-finding instruments, radio compasses, altimeters, and other flight instruments; he also requested permission to evaluate new types of aircraft for night operations. Pilot Wesley Smith also noted, "We need a beacon ray that will penetrate storms and guide us to the fields in bad weather."[1]

Left: A Ford 5-AT-C Trimotor NC-8410 and a Hamilton H-47 Metal Plane NC-69E share a maintenance facility at St. Paul, Minnesota, circa 1932. Between them is a Waco Taperwing, which was used for night mail. Northwest Airlines/Noel Allard Collection

Right: Wesley Smith at Hadley Field, New Jersey, 1924. He flew the air mail on the famous 1921 experimental night flights and also the first leg of the 1924 experimental day-and-night transcontinental schedules. By that time he and E. Hamilton Lee were the senior pilots of the Air Mail Service. Jesse Davidson Aviation Archives

E. Hamilton Lee in 1921. He was a flying instructor for the U.S. Army during World War I and then one of the first air mail pilots. Later he flew for United Airlines, logging more than four million miles during his career. Jesse Davidson Aviation Archives

Opposite: *On August 10, 1920, this Martin MP aircraft was the first air mail plane to land at Minneapolis on a route test.* Metropolitan Airports Commission/Noel Allard Collection

178 ▶ The Airlines Are Born

Sacks of mail being loaded into a Northwest Airways SB-1 Detroiter at St. Paul Minnesota. Date unknown. Clerk Fred Fischer is handing the air mail to Pilot Charles "Speed" Holman. Holman was the chief pilot and an aerial stuntman in his spare time. He later died stunting in 1931. Jim Borden Collection

Opposite: *Mail being unloaded from a NAT Douglas M-4 aircraft in the mid-1920s. Note firearms for security.*
©Museum of Flight

In June 1929, pilot Edwin H. Middaugh lost one of his Ford Trimotor's engines on takeoff from St. Paul and crash-landed in Indian Mounds Park. He was the only fatality on that flight and the first one for Northwest Airlines in a million passenger miles. Noel Allard Collection

As night service was introduced to the route through the Allegheny Mountains, beacons and emergency landing fields became a top priority. The eastern terminus of that route was moved from Hazelhurst, New York, to Hadley Field, near New Brunswick, New Jersey. Pilots would no longer have to cope with the fog and industrial smoke and haze of New York City. Mail trains were used to expedite the movement of mail between New York City's General Post Office and Hadley Field.

In the West also, the air mail system was being developed. In July 1926, Western Express was established in Sacramento, California, to link the vast open spaces of the West to the main trunk line of the Air Mail Service. The new company wanted the Los Angeles–Las Vegas–Salt Lake City route and had serious backing. It succeeded in acquiring the route. To lay out the route for Western Express, Al DeGarmo, a Varney employee, took a couple of Dodge panel trucks and loaded them with rolls of canvas two feet wide. We then spent two weeks driving over the L.A. to Salt Lake [route], camping out at night and cooking for ourselves. When we found a level place where we thought we'd be able to manage a forced landing, we would unroll enough canvas to help us spot it from the air. We'd make a "V" with the canvas to tell us which way to land.[2]

DeGarmo also formed the canvas into a "T" at certain spots, which meant that a pilot could try to land but probably would not be able to take off.[3]

By 1927, the government was anxious to turn the transcontinental route over to private carriers. Postmaster General Harry New awarded the Chicago–San Francisco route to Boeing Transport, but he delayed a decision on the eastern route after North American Airways (in which several pilots had a financial interest) underbid National Air Transport (NAT).[4] NAT had more political clout and in the end won the contract.

Opposite: On June 7, 1926, savage winds brought down this Partridge-Keller biplane in a field just south of the Minneapolis airport. The pilot, Elmer Lee Partridge, was carrying air mail to Chicago. He died in the accident, but his load of air mail survived and was put on a train to Chicago. Jim Borden/Noel Allard Collection

A Stinson SB-1 Detroiter C-872 on skis at St. Paul Airport, 1926. As soon as Northwest Airways incorporated, it purchased four Detroiters from Eddie Stinson to begin air mail flights between the Twin Cities (Minneapolis and St. Paul) and Chicago. Northwest Airlines/Noel Allard Collection

Opposite: A Boeing four-passenger Model 40B-4 mail plane flying by Mt. Rainier's summit 14,408 feet above sea level. Date unknown. This aircraft had a service ceiling of 16,100 feet and could carry one pilot, four passengers, and 500 pounds of air mail. Jesse Davidson Aviation Archives

This Boeing Model 80 aircraft was introduced in 1929 to carry not only mail but passengers as well. With this aircraft, United Airlines established a 27-hour coast-to-coast service. It dwarfs what appears to be an Aeronca C-2 aircraft (left). Jim Ruotsala

Opposite: Charles Lindbergh when he was an air mail pilot. After surviving four parachute jumps from disabled air mail aircraft, Lindbergh earned the nickname "Lucky Lindy." Date and location unknown. Jesse Davidson Aviation Archives

By fall 1927, the Air Mail Service was history. The government sold most of its assets to the carriers, and the Commerce Department acquired the extensive radio station network, beacons, and navigational aids. The pilots and support personnel who had served with the former Air Mail Service went to both Boeing and NAT (which later would become United Airlines).

When Charles Lindbergh conquered the Atlantic in May 1927 with his epic New York–Paris flight, he turned America on to aviation. Every young man wanted to be a pilot. Lindbergh noted about his flight, "It was like a match lighting a bonfire. I thought thereafter that people confused the light of the bonfire with the flame of the match, and that one individual was credited with doing what, in reality, many groups of individuals had done."[5]

By 1930, the government had decided the carriers should transport passengers and freight, and it rented space on them for air mail. This move encouraged manufacturers to develop larger multiengine aircraft. In the meantime, the carriers switched to Ford Trimotors, Tri-Stinsons, Curtiss Condors, Boeings 80s, and multiengine Fokkers. The larger operators could afford the biggest aircraft and were awarded the longest routes.

On August 25, 1930, American Airways was awarded the southern transcontinental route. Western Express merged with Transcontinental Air Transport to become what eventually was called TWA and flew the central transcontinental route. Boeing merged with NAT to become known as United Airlines and fly the northern transcontinental route.

The Airlines Are Born

This Boeing Model 221 aircraft, introduced in 1930, had a 575-horsepower engine and could carry six people and 800 pounds of mail and freight. The model 221A could carry eight passengers. Northeastern Nevada Museum

Left: United Airlines air mail schedule from January 1933. ©Museum of Flight

Opposite: The Stearman LT-1 aircraft (right) was ideal for carrying the air mail. Powered by a Pratt & Whitney 525-horsepower engine, it had a payload of 1,270 pounds and could also carry four passengers in front. It also was set up for radio and night/instrument flying. Maintenance was simplified by making the cowling relatively easy to remove. Three LT-1s were delivered to Interstate Airlines in 1929. The LT-1 was quite similar to the Douglas M-2 series aircraft, except that it had a four-seat cabin instead of a front mail pit or cockpit.
Jesse Davidson Aviation Archives

188 ▶ THE AIRLIINES ARE BORN

The industry was developing more modern equipment. Biplanes were no longer in vogue. The all-metal twin-engine Boeing 247 could carry ten passengers and the mail. In 1933, Donald Douglas designed and built the first model of a long and very successful DC series all-metal aircraft. The DC-1 and DC-2 came with twin engines, full flaps, and variable pitch props. On one TWA flight over the Alleghenies, a Douglas DC-2 averaged 230 miles per hour and topped a storm at 19,500 feet.[6] Modern jet airliners can fly more than twice as fast as that Douglas DC-2 and can go over storms more than twice as high as it could.

On June 25, 1936, the Douglas DC-3 entered service and quickly established itself as a versatile workhorse for the airlines. With a lengthened fuselage, broader wing span, and increased seat capacity (twenty-eight passengers), it served in varied civilian and military missions all over the world. With a maximum takeoff weight of 28,000 pounds and a range of 1,025 miles, the DC-3 was ideal for hauling cargo, mail, and passengers. When production of this type ended in 1947, 10,654 civil and military variants had been delivered.

U.S. airlines not only developed from contract air mail carriers, but they also owed their heritage to the brave aerial postmen who often put their lives on the line as they piloted sometimes-unreliable aircraft in extreme weather conditions—and flew on a wing and a prayer. "The story of the airplane and the air mail is the story of the beginnings of global communication, an earlier step in our awakening to each other. It is also part of the ever-old and ever-new story of men in process … of men finding out who they are by leaping into the unknown."[7]

In the 1920s, NAT Airliines produced this decal to promote its Travel Air Model 5000 aircraft for carrying both passengers and air mail. ©Museum of Flight

Opposite: Several different NAT aircraft awaiting their air mail shipments and perhaps a weather break on a wintry day. Date and location unknown. ©Museum of Flight

This NAT air mail aircraft was the first Curtiss Carrier Pigeon built. It was first used on the Chicago-Dallas CAM route in 1927. It had a top speed of 130 mph and was one of the first air mail aircraft to have a payload of 1,000 pounds. A later model, with a 600-horsepower Curtiss engine, had a payload of 3,300 pounds. ©Museum of Flight

Opposite: In the 1920s, several Travel Air 5000 five-seat aircraft were built for NAT Airlines. They met the requirements of the Department of Commerce and were ahead of their time. These aircraft had Wright J-5 engines and were developed by Clyde Cessna, Lloyd Stearman, and Walter Beech (all three of whom went on to design and manufacture some of the world's best general aviation aircraft and military trainers). ©Museum of Flight

A NAT Airlines Travel Air 5000 with a load of mail landing at Hadley Field in New Brunswick, New Jersey. Date unknown. ©Museum of Flight

Opposite: Two Boeing Air Transport aircraft (left foreground), meeting NAT aircraft, in rear, for air mail exchange at Chicago. Date unknown. ©Museum of Flight

Jack Knight
1938

Opposite: Jack Knight set the standard for air mail pilots, but he also went on to become one of the longest tenured United Airline pilots. In this photo, taken in 1938, at Dearborn, Michigan, he is standing in front of one of the Boeing Model 40B-2 aircraft he flew in the 1930s. United Airlines

Jack Knight (above) in front of one of United Airline's Douglas DC-3s. He retired in 1937 after flying more than 417,000 air route miles for the Air Mail Service (for Boeing Air Transport and United Airlines). By 1938 the DC-3 hauled 95% of all U.S. airline traffic and was the major air mail carrier in the United States. United Airlines

An American Airlines Douglas DC-3 aircraft in flight. Date and location unknown. Powered by two 900-horsepower Wright Cyclone engines, this workhorse normally could cruise at 185 miles per hour and climb over inclement weather. It also had "George," a revolutionary auto pilot developed by the Sperry Gyroscope Company. And for redundancy, there were two sets of instruments in the cockpit, each independent of the other in case one had any problems.
Jesse Davidson Aviation Archives

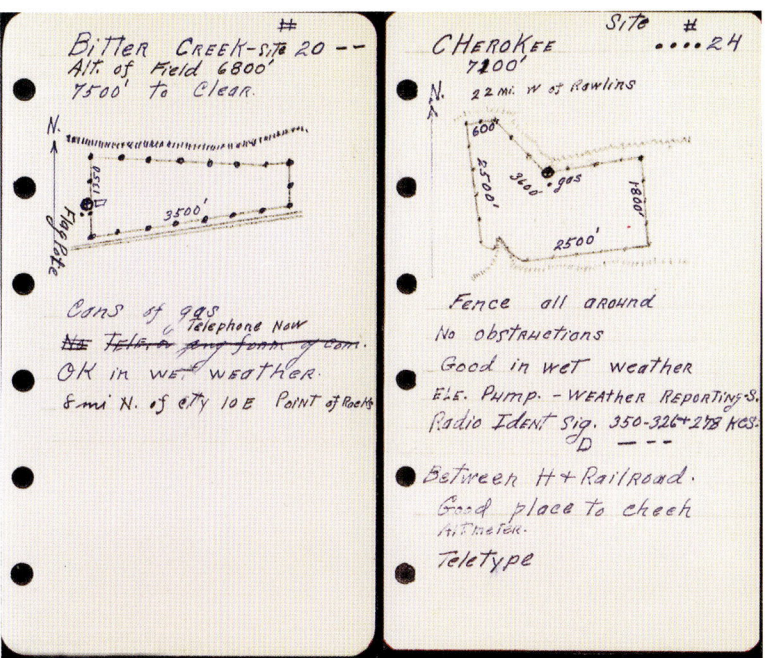

Above: Pages from Elray Jeppesen's "Little Black Book." These notes eventually evolved into the instrument approach plates, which to this day are published by the company Jeppesen founded. Many pilots all over the world use Jeppesen approach plates and en route charts.
©Museum of Flight

Right: Elray Jeppesen at the controls of a Boeing Model 80A in 1930. Jeppesen played a key role in the development of instrument charts and approach plates that pilots use for flights in instrument conditions.
©Museum of Flight

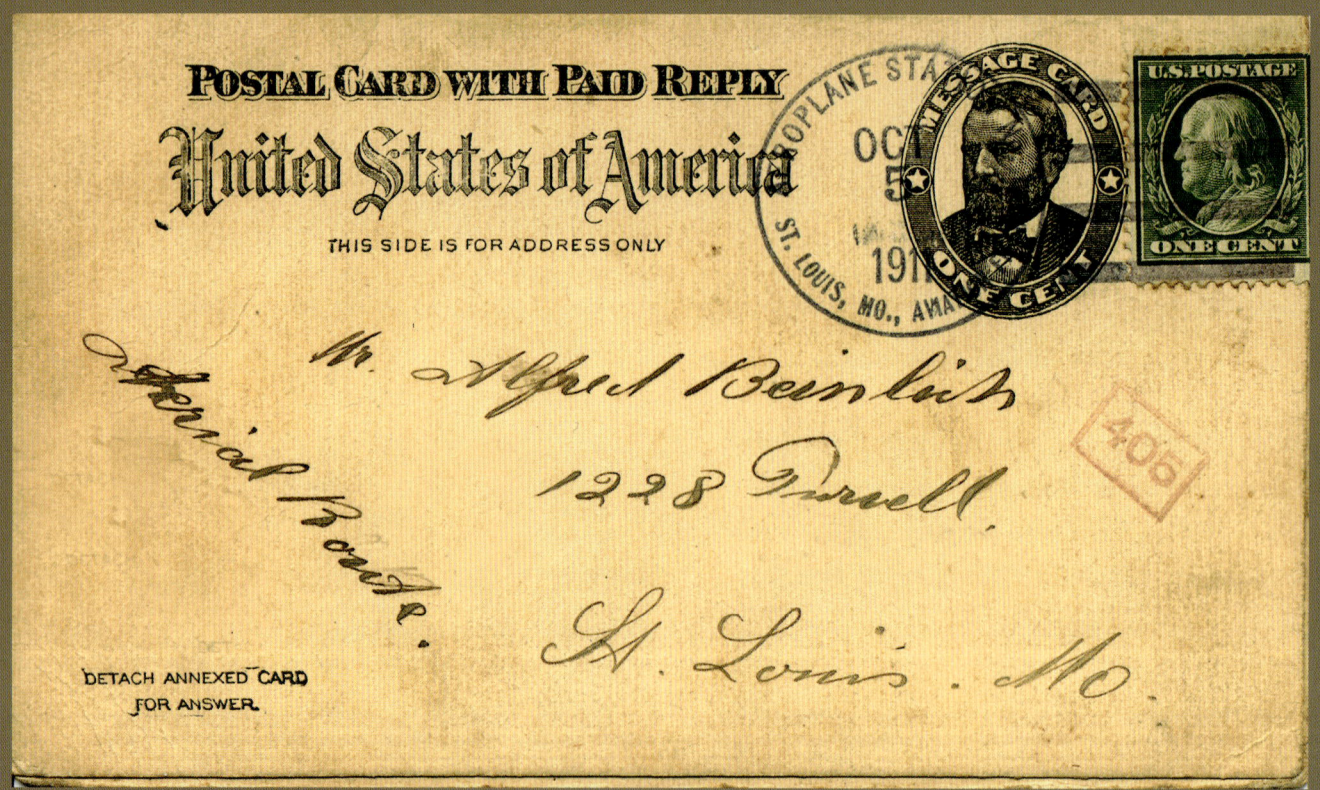

CHAPTER 15
Air Mail First-Day Covers

Special postmarks were placed on air mail first-day covers (envelopes) on flights originating from cities across the United States, starting in 1911. By the time the United States entered World War I in 1917, close to seventy different air mail postmarks had been developed and used.

Some air mail first-day covers contain the signatures of the pilot, which make them even more collectible and interesting. For some historic flights—such as the first experimental air mail flight in Alaska on February 2, 1924—there are no known surviving first-day air mail covers.

Air mail first-day postal covers chronicle the rich history of the U.S. Air Mail Service. From the very first 43,000 pieces of air mail flown in fixed wing aircraft by Earle Ovington and his fellow designated air mail pilots, H. H. "Hap" Arnold and Eugene Ely, to the advent of priority mail, the covers trace the development of air mail routes all over the United States and celebrate aviation milestones. *Note: In captions, the abbreviation FDC means first-day cover (envelope). All air mail first-day postal covers courtesy of Bruce McAllister.*

Opposite: This rare postal card has an October 5, 1911, cancellation, the day on which some 25,000 letters and postcards were the first flown by air mail west of the Mississippi. From October 4 to October 8, 1911, air mail was flown from Kinloch Field, near St. Louis to Fairgrounds Park near downtown St. Louis for re-dispatch.

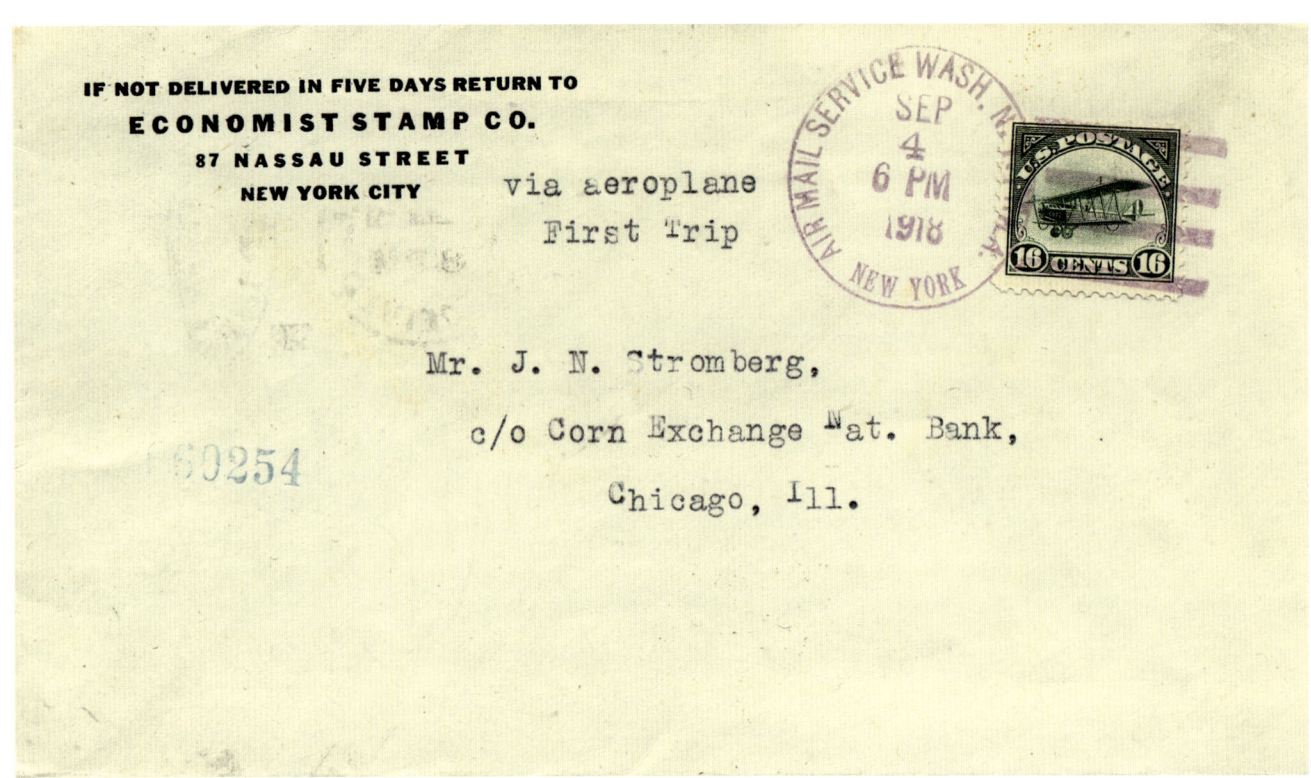

A rare September 4, 1918, FDC. This letter was in one of the air mail bags carried by Max Miller on a test flight to examine the feasibility of long distance air mail. Miller arrived in Chicago two days later, landing at Grant Park at 7:08 p.m., thirty-seven hours after departing from New York. The back of the envelope had a train cancellation on the back indicating its last leg was by train and it arrived in Chicago at 7:05 p.m. on September 6. Donald Holmes, author of Air Mail—An Illustrated History, *looked at this FDC and believes the "train late" notation on the back of the envelope signifies that in fact the plane was late and the post office had to acknowledge that it arrived after business hours. Ed Gardner, flying the other air mail on this experimental flight, had tail skid problems, could not keep up with Miller, and arrived in Chicago at 6:30 a.m. on September 7.*

An August 22, 1923, FDC that went by night air mail from New York to Los Angeles.

This FDC was flown via night air mail to Chicago on CAM Route No. 9 on May 29, 1926. The originating post office cancellation not clear and this CAM route was not inaugurated until June 7, 1926. CAM Route No. 9 was between Minneapolis and Chicago.

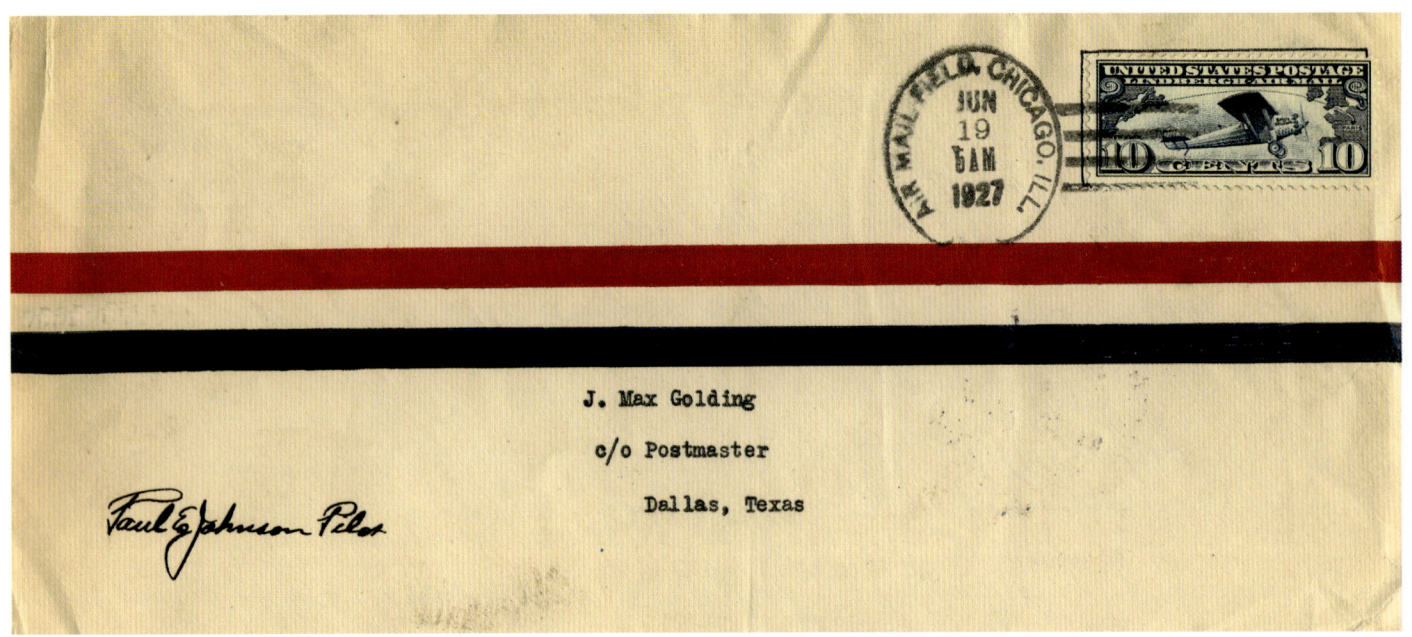

Above: An FDC, June 19, 1927, signed by Air Mail pilot Paul E. Johnson.

An 1927 Lindbergh celebration FDC.

A first-day cover on CAM Route 27 between Cleveland and Chicago, 1929, signed by pilot Ralph DeVore.

A first-day cover celebrating the first official aerial air mail pickup at Youngstown, Ohio. With the Adams nonstop method, the aircraft would fly close to the ground to catch a mailbag suspended between two poles set sixty feet apart.

AIR MAIL FIRST-DAY COVERS

Two unusual cancellation "strikes" on an 1930 FDC cover.

An October 25, 1930, FDC on CAM Route 34 between Amarillo and Chicago, celebrating the first flight between New York to Los Angeles.

An FDC celebrating twenty years of air mail service, May 14, 1938. By 1938, the DC-3 aircraft shown on envelope, was the workhorse for the airlines. Pavois ©S-MCO

A 1941 FDC celebrating twenty years of air mail service. ©Art Craft

An FDC promoting in-flight processing of air mail. Note the American Airlines logo within the cachet.

Below: A five-cent Air Mail FDC promoting helicopters for regional postal service in New York. ©PentArts

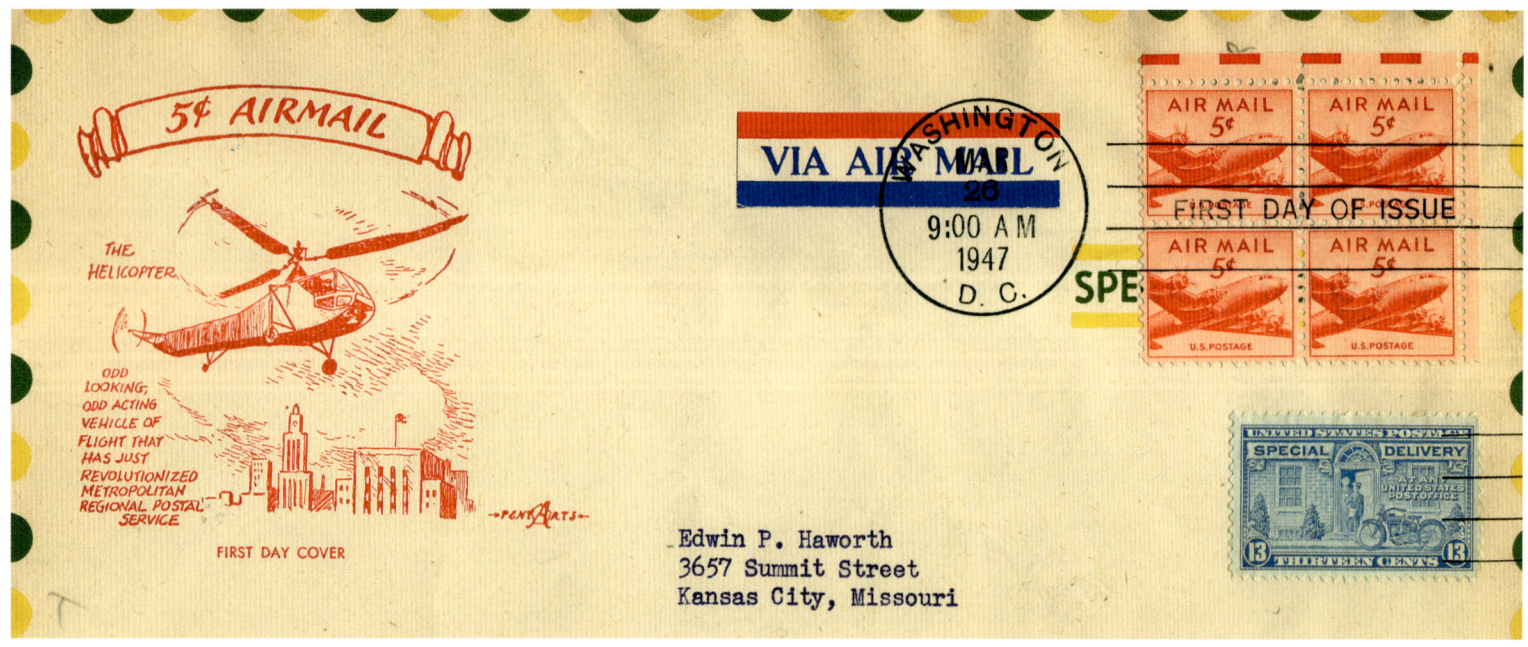

208 ➤ Air Mail First-Day Covers

Notes

Introduction
[1] Donald B. Holmes, *Air Mail—An Illustrated History,* p. 9.
[2] Ibid., p. 13.
[3] Ibid., p. 16.
[4] Dale Nielson, ed., *Saga of the U.S. Air Mail Service, 1918–1927,* p. 3.
[5] Letter from Donald B. Holmes to Bruce McAllister, November 3, 2002.
[6] Benjamin Lipsner, *The AirMail—Jennies to Jets,* p. 167.
[7] Ibid., p. 165.
[8] Dean Smith, *By the Seat of My Pants,* p. 132.
[9] Keith Lambertsen interview by Bruce McAllister, November 20, 2002.
[10] William Leary, ed., reprint of *Pilots' Directions,* p. 35.
[11] Jesse Davidson Papers.

Chapter 1
[1] William Leary, *Aerial Pioneers,* pp. 16–17.
[2] Ibid., p. 14.
[3] Jesse Davidson Papers.
[4] Ibid.
[5] Ibid.
[6] Ibid.

Chapter 2
[1] Donald B. Holmes, *Air Mail—An Illustrated History,* p. 73.
[2] Debra L. Winegarten, *Katherine Stinson,* p. 12.
[3] *Helena Independent,* September 22, 1933.
[4] Debra L. Winegarten, *Katherine Stinson,* p. 24.
[5] *Helena Independent,* September 22, 1933.
[6] Debra L. Winegarten, *Katherine Stinson,* p. 29.
[7] Ibid., p. 31.
[8] *Handbook of Texas Online* (www.tsha.utexas.edu), p. 2 (Stinson article).
[9] Debra L. Winegarten, *Katherine Stinson,* p. 54.
[10] *Handbook of Texas Online,* p. 2.

Chapter 3
[1] Michael Taylor, ed., *Jane's Encyclopedia of Aviation,* p. 281.
[2] Air Mail Pioneer Website (www.airmailpioneers.org): Reuben Fleet profile.
[3] Donald B. Holmes, *Air Mail—An Illustrated History,* p. 92.
[4] Donald Jackson, *Flying the Mail,* p. 28.
[5] Ibid.

Chapter 4
[1] Donald Jackson, *Flying the Mail,* p. 29.
[2] Donald B. Holmes, *Air Mail—An Illustrated History,* p. 104.
[3] Page Shamburger, *Tracks Across the Sky,* p. 37.
[4] Copy of original letter in Jesse Davidson Papers.

Chapter 5
[1] Jesse Davidson Papers.
[2] Ibid.
[3] Ibid.
[4] Ibid.
[5] Ibid.
[6] Ibid.
[7] Ibid.

Chapter 7
[1] Dean Smith, *By the Seat of My Pants,* p. 169.
[2] Ibid., p. 171.
[3] Page Shamburger, *Tracks Across the Sky,* p. 31.
[4] Jesse Davidson Papers.
[5] Ibid.

Chapter 8
[1] Donald B. Holmes, *Air Mail—An Illustrated History,* p. 113.
[2] Dean Smith, *By the Seat of My Pants,* p. 115.
[3] William Leary, ed., *Pilots' Directions,* p. 16.
[4] Benjamin Lipsner, *The AirMail—Jennies to Jets,* p. 194.
[5] William Leary, ed., *Pilots' Directions,* pp. 16–17.

Chapter 9
[1] Donald B. Holmes, *Air Mail—An Illustrated History,* p. 135.
[2] Jean Potter, *The Flying North,* p. 4.
[3] As quoted in Dorothy Page, *Polar Pilot,* p. 158.
[4] Ibid., p. 6.
[5] Eileen Mork, interviewed by Bruce McAllister, June 30, 2003.
[6] Dorothy Page, *Polar Pilot,* p. 17.
[7] Eileen Mork, interviewed by Bruce McAllister, June 30, 2003.

Chapter 10
[1] "Stories of Early Air Mail Days—and Nights," *U.S. Air Services,* November 1953, p. 10.
[2] Excerpts from Joe V. Magee letter to Jesse Davidson, July 4, 1954.

Chapter 11
[1] Dean Smith, *By the Seat of My Pants*, p. 132.
[2] Donald Jackson, *Flying the Mail*, p. 58.
[3] Dean Smith, *By the Seat of My Pants*, pp. 133–134.
[4] Ibid., p. 134.
[5] Earl Shobe interview by Bruce McAllister, December 11, 2002.

Chapter 12
[1] Peter M. Bowers, *Boeing Aircraft Since 1916*, p. 37.
[2] Ibid., p. 40.
[3] Jim Brown, *Hubbard: The Forgotten Boeing Aviator*, p. 34.
[4] Ibid., p. 38.

Chapter 13
[1] Donald B. Holmes, *Air Mail—An Illustrated History*, p. 146.
[2] Ibid., p. 146.
[3] Ibid., p. 147.

Chapter 14
[1] William Leary, *Aerial Pioneers*, pp. 216–217.
[2] Donald B. Holmes, *Air Mail—An Illustrated History*, p. 151.
[3] Ibid., p. 152.
[4] William Leary, *Aerial Pioneers*, p. 236.
[5] Charles Lindbergh, *Autobiography of Values*, p. 310.
[6] Page Shamburger, *Tracks Across the Sky*, p. 151.
[7] Robert G. Blakesley quote from Donald B. Holmes, *Air Mail—An Illustrated History*, p. 216.

Bibliography

BOOKS

Allard, Noel, and Gerald Sandvick, *Minnesota Aviation History, 1857–1945*. MAHB Publishing, Chaska, MN, 1993

Berg, A. Scott, *Lindbergh*. G. P. Putnam's Sons, New York, 1998

Borden, Norman E., Jr., *Air Mail Emergency, 1934*. Bond Wheelwright, Freeport, ME, 1968

Bowers, Peter M., *Boeing Aircraft Since 1916*. Aero Publishers, Fallbrook, CA, 1966

Boyne, Walter J., *De Havilland DH 4: From Flaming Coffin to Living Legend*. Smithsonian Institution Press, Washington, DC, 1984

Brown, Jim, *Hubbard: The Forgotten Boeing Aviator*. Peanut Butter Publishing, Seattle, WA, 1996

Bryan, C. D. B., *The National Air and Space Museum*. Harry N. Abrams, New York, 1979

Chatfield, Charles, and Charles Taylor, *The Airplane and Its Engine*. McGraw Hill, New York, 1928

Dickey, Phillip S., III, *The Liberty Engine, 1918–1942*. Smithsonian Institution Press, Washington, DC, 1968

Dixon, Franklin W., *Over the Rockies with the Air Mail*. Grosset & Dunlap, New York, 1927

Glines, Carroll V., *Polar Aviation*. Franklin Watts, New York, 1964

Glines, Carroll V., *The Saga of the Air Mail*. D. Van Nostrand, Princeton, NJ, 1968

Haller, Stephen A., *The Last Word in Airfields—San Francisco's Crissy Field*. Golden Gate National Parks Association, San Francisco, 2001

Holmes, Donald B., *Air Mail—An Illustrated History*. Clarkson N. Potter, New York, 1981

Jackson, Donald D., *Flying the Mail*. Time-Life Books, Alexandria, VA, 1982

Komon, Nick A., *Bonfires to Beacons*. Smithsonian Institution Press, Washington, DC, 1989. (Originally published by U.S. Dept. of Transportation, FAA)

Kronstein, Max, *Pioneer Airpost Flights of the World*. American Air Mail Society, Washington, DC, 1978

Leary, William M., *Aerial Pioneers—The U.S. Air Mail Service, 1918–1927*. Smithsonian Institution Press, Washington, DC, 1985

Leary, William M., ed., *Pilots' Directions—The Transcontinental Airway and Its History*. University of Iowa Press, Iowa City, 1990

Lindbergh, Charles, *Autobiography of Values*. Harcourt, Brace & Jovanovich, New York, 1977

Lipsner, Benjamin B., *The AirMail—Jennies to Jets*. Wilcox & Follett, Chicago, 1951

Mackay, James, *Airmails, 1870–1970*. B.T. Batsford Ltd., London, 1971

Nielson, Dale, ed., *Saga of the U.S. Air Mail Service, 1918-1927*. Air Mail Pioneers, San Francisco, CA, 1962

Page, Dorothy, *Polar Pilot*. Interstate Publishers, Danville, IL, 1992

Palmer, Henry, Jr., *This Was Air Travel*. Superior Publishing, Seattle, WA, 1960

Potter, Jean. *The Flying North*. MacMillan, New York, 1955

Ross, Walter S., *The Last Hero: Charles A. Lindbergh*. Harper & Row, New York, 1964

St.-Exupery, Antoine, *Night Flight*. Century Company, New York, 1932

Scott 2002 Specialized Catalogue of United States Stamps and Covers. Scott Publishing, Sidney, OH, 2001

Shamburger, Page, *Tracks Across the Sky: The Story of the Pioneers of the U.S. Air Mail*. J. B. Lippincott, New York, 1964

Smith, Dean C., *By the Seat of My Pants*. Little, Brown, Boston, 1961

Sunderman, James F., *Early Air Pioneers*. Franklin Watts, New York, 1961

Taylor, John, and Kenneth Munson, *History of Aviation*. Crown Publishers, New York, 1972

Taylor, Michael, ed., *Jane's Encyclopedia of Aviation*. Portland House, New York, 1989

Taylor, Poyntz, *Airways of America*. H. W. Wilson, New York, 1958

Theiss, Lewis E., *Piloting the U.S. Air Mail*. W. A. Wilde, Boston, 1927

Whitehouse, Arch, *The Sky's the Limit*. MacMillan, New York, 1971

Winegarten, Debra L., *Katherine Stinson, The Flying Schoolgirl*. Eakin Press, Austin, TX, 2000

MAGAZINE ARTICLES

"Aviation in Alaska: The Pioneer Days," *Alaska Geographic*, Vol. 25, No. 4, 1998, pp. 13–14

"On the Trail of the Air Mail," *National Geographic*, January 1926, pp. 1–61

"Stories of Early Air Mail Days—and Nights," *U.S. Air Mail Services*, November 1953, pp. 7–10, 21–22

A longtime resident of the Colorado Rockies, **Bruce McAllister** is a pilot and semi-retired freelance magazine photographer who has logged many of his 4,800 hours of flight time in Alaska and Canada. His previous books, *Wings Above the Arctic* and *Wings Over the Alaska Highway* (with Peter Corley-Smith) have received acclaim for their photography and unusual stories.

Jesse Davidson (1913-1983) developed an interest in aviation at an early age and eventually became an aviation editor in New York City. He was the lead consultant of Time-Life's book, *Flying The Mail*, and had a passion for collecting early air mail photographs, letters, and interviews of some of the original U.S. air mail pilots.